COMMODORE 64
BASIC PROGRAMS IN MINUTES

COMMODORE 64™
BASIC PROGRAMS IN MINUTES

STANLEY R. TROST

[redacted]

[redacted]

SYBEX®

BERKELEY • PARIS • DÜSSELDORF

Cover art by Jean-François Pénichoux
Design by Nina Hoecker

Library of Congress Card Number: 83-51192
ISBN 0-89588-154-3
Printed in the United States of America
10 9 8 7 6 5 4 3 2 1

ACKNOWLEDGEMENTS

Many people contributed ideas and hard work to this book. Rudolph Langer suggested the book and pointed the way to a number of improvements. David Lichtblau provided valuable assistance with program development and verification. Barbara Gordon and Joel Kreisman edited the manuscript, checked the programs, and prepared the programs for production. Many other members of the SYBEX staff were also part of the team that put this book together.

Stan Trost
September 1983

CONTENTS

APPENDICES

PREFACE

Commodore 64 BASIC Programs in Minutes will help you discover the full power and flexibility of your Commodore 64 computer. This book contains more than 65 practical programs and subroutines that are fully tested and ready to run; they provide a wide variety of business, personal, and educational applications. You do not need to understand the BASIC programming language to use these programs; you just enter them into your computer and use them for your own applications.

These programs will help you make important financial decisions; for example, you can find the break-even point of a new business, calculate the monthly payment necessary to establish a college fund for your children, and find the future value of regular deposits in an individual retirement account (IRA). The record keeping programs allow you to create a mailing list, phone directory, and automobile log. Students and nonstudents alike will find the mathematics practice programs especially useful. These practice programs help sharpen arithmetic skills; they can also help students with homework assignments.

Commodore 64 BASIC Programs in Minutes contains a number of unique programs. The fraction practice programs, long multiplication drill, record keeping programs, and combined data analysis and graphing programs are seldom found in a collection of programs.

The use of standard subroutines is also unique. A primary goal of this book is to provide programs that are *short* and easy to enter in your computer. To achieve this goal, the programs were created using a standard set of programs as subroutines. These subroutines will also save you a great deal of effort when you create your own programs.

This book does not teach BASIC language programming; however, use of the programs will help you understand BASIC in a painless, almost automatic way. As you become familiar with BASIC, you will be able to modify the programs in this book and create new programs.

Let's now review the contents of the book. Chapter 1 gives instructions for using the programs and reviews the interactive features built into them. You should read this chapter before you use the programs.

Chapter 2 is a set of programs for home and business finance. It includes programs that calculate the compound interest you earn in a bank, the future value of regular savings deposits (for example, the future value of deposits in an IRA), the interest rate earned on an investment, and the time required to double your money. These programs can help you make many important investment decisions.

Chapter 3 contains a collection of business programs. These programs compute depreciation, the break-even point for a new business, wages earned with overtime, and decision analysis. The business programs will be helpful to business people, employees, and consumers.

In Chapter 4 we present real estate application programs including mortgage payment calculation, balloon payment calculation, and rental property analysis. You will, for example, be able to find the interest you can save by increasing your monthly house payment. Investors, homeowners, and prospective homeowners will find these programs helpful.

Chapter 5 includes a set of data analysis programs that can be used to analyze both scientific and financial data. The programs can compute mean and standard deviation, various moving averages, and linear regression, and they can graph the results. These programs can be of use in analyzing and projecting stock market trends, among other things.

Chapter 6 contains a set of record keeping programs to keep personal and automobile records. With these programs you will be able to use your computer to keep mailing lists and phone directories as well as mileage records for your car. The programs are designed to be modified easily for other applications.

Chapter 7 presents a number of useful arithmetic drills for students of all grade levels and abilities. These drills include addition, subtraction, multiplication, and division, using whole numbers as well as fractions. These programs can help sharpen your math skills and even help with homework!

We also include two appendices with this book. Appendix A lists the standard subroutines that enable the programs within the chapters to be so short. Their functions are described in REM statements. These subroutines are in numerical order so that you can easily refer to them. Appendix B shows you how to use these subroutines to create your own programs. Descriptions and examples are provided.

1

INTRODUCTION

This chapter shows you how *Commodore 64 BASIC Programs in Minutes* can greatly increase your computer's effectiveness. You will learn how to enter and run programs, create a subroutine library, and build a library of related programs that can run from a menu. You will also learn what interactive program design means and how it is accomplished in these programs.

The programs in this book do not require knowledge of the BASIC programming language. They can simply be used as is to solve a wide variety of business, home, and education problems. However, if you wish to expand your programming knowledge, these programs will show you how to take full advantage of the powerful features of your computer.

HOW TO START

You will need a Commodore 64 computer and a cassette recorder or disk drive. (The disk drive is required to run the programs in Chapter 6.) The programs in this book are written in CBM BASIC. Review your Commodore 64 manual for detailed instructions on running BASIC.

To start BASIC, simply turn on the power. After a short pause the screen displays the cursor:

```
READY
■
```

You will need two cassette tapes or two formatted disks (formatting instructions are in the Commodore disk manual) to save the programs you enter (one as a master and one as a backup). You should always make two copies of every program.

At this point you can enter any of the programs in this book. You enter a program by typing the lines in the program listings exactly as they appear in this book. After each line press the return key. Let's enter the following program:

```
100 PRINT "HELLO"
110 END
```

Begin by typing the first line (100 PRINT "HELLO"). Enter this line by striking the return key. Complete the program entry by typing and entering the second line.

You will sometimes make mistakes in entering the programs. Short lines are easily corrected by retyping the entire line. The Commodore manual explains other methods you can use to correct errors on longer lines.

To run this program, type RUN 100 and strike the return key. Notice the display on your screen; your program has printed HELLO below the program you entered. We'll give you more information on entering, saving, and running the programs later in this chapter.

REMARK STATEMENTS

We use *remarks* to make the programs easier to understand. Remark statements begin with the symbol REM. In Figure 1.1, remarks make a

```
100 REM --------------
101 N$="SAMPLE PROGRAM"
102 REM --------------
110 INPUT X
120 INPUT Y
130 PRINT X+Y: REM PRINT THE SUM OF X AND Y
140 END
```

Figure 1.1: Program Listing Including Remarks

```
100 REM
101 N$="SAMPLE PROGRAM"
110 INPUT X
120 INPUT Y
130 PRINT X+Y
140 END
```

Figure 1.2: Program Listing with Remarks Condensed

border at the top of the program and explain the action of line 130. With one exception, you don't have to type the remarks as you enter the programs. The exception is that you must type the word REM on the first line of the program. The first REM is necessary because of the design of our programs. Figure 1.2 shows the same program listing after you type the necessary lines.

BUILDING A SUBROUTINE LIBRARY

The programs in this book use a central subroutine library to simplify program entry and output formatting. A *subroutine* is simply a program that is used as part of another program. For example, one central subroutine handles data entry for many of our programs. These subroutines allow our programs to be short and therefore easy for you to enter.

Appendix A contains the program listings for the subroutines you will use in this book. Appendix B shows you how to use some of these subroutines to create your own programs.

Before you enter the programs in this book, you must build the subroutine library. Turn to Appendix A, where you will find the instructions for the standard subroutines. All readers must enter the subroutines beginning with lines 3400, 4200, 5000, 5400, 6200, 6600, 7000, 7400, and 7800. Readers using a disk drive must also enter the programs beginning with lines 3000 and 3800.

Begin with the subroutine at line 3400. First type NEW to clear any old programs from the computer; then type the instructions for this subroutine into your computer. (Remember that remarks are not entered except in the first line.) Your entry should match that shown in Figure 1.3.

```
3400 REM
3420 Q1$="WOULD  YOU LIKE TO"
3430 Q3$="AGAIN  Y OR N ?"
3440 GOSUB 5000
3450 GOSUB 7800
3460 RETURN
```

Figure 1.3: Program Listing: ANOTH Subroutine

Continue to enter the rest of the subroutines. After you enter the standard routines, save them on tape or disk. Follow the instructions in the Commodore manual to ready your tape or disk. To save the subroutines on tape, type

```
SAVE "SUBLIB"
```

To save them on disk, type

```
SAVE "SUBLIB", 8
```

Your central subroutine library is now stored with the file name SUBLIB. You will merge SUBLIB with your application programs as you build the applications.

ENTERING AND RUNNING THE PROGRAMS

You are now ready to enter a program. Begin by loading the subroutine library. Type

```
LOAD "SUBLIB"
```

(from tape) or

```
LOAD "SUBLIB", 8
```

(from disk). Then type the program instructions as they are shown in the program listings. The programs in Chapters 2, 3, 4, and 5 should be saved in one file for each chapter. (Use file names that are meaningful to you.) The programs can then be run by loading the file for the desired chapter, then typing RUN and the first line number of the desired program. When you have typed in all the programs in a chapter, you can create a menu to run the programs in that chapter. A *menu* is a list of programs that you use to select the program you want to run. Instructions for creating the menu are given in each chapter. The programs within each chapter begin with unique line numbers; this allows you to store the programs and menu for each chapter together in one file.

For example, Chapter 2 contains a number of programs that are useful when you make financial calculations. Load your subroutine library, type in the Future Value of a Deposit program, and save them both on disk or tape by typing

```
SAVE "FIN"
```

(for tape) or

```
SAVE "FIN", 8
```

(for disk). When you need another financial program, load the first financial program you saved by typing

```
LOAD "FIN"
```

(for tape) or

```
LOAD "FIN", 8
```

(for disk). Now you can type in another financial program, for example, the Time to Double program. Save both programs together by typing

```
SAVE "FIN"
```

or

```
SAVE "FIN", 8
```

You can see how this method enables you to build a library of financial programs.

The Financial Programs Menu enables you to run any program in that chapter by selecting it from the menu—no more line numbers to remember. To activate the menu program you should replace the END command in the last line of each program with a RETURN command.

The programs in Chapters 5–7 are entered in a slightly different way. They begin rather than end with a menu program, so in these chapters you first enter the menu and then the application program you choose. The programs are run by selecting them from the menu. Because we place the menus at the beginning of each set of programs in these chapters, you don't have to bother with replacing any END statements in the programs.

INTERACTIVE FEATURES

The word *interactive* refers to the interaction between the computer, the programs, and the user. The goal of an interactive program is to make it easy for the user to interact with the computer.

We accomplish this goal in various ways. When possible, we answer questions with a single keystroke that doesn't require the return key. For example, programs are selected from the menus with a single digit, and yes/no questions require simply a Y or an N. Another interactive feature we use is to place all questions at the bottom of the screen, so you can always look for them in the same place. Your answers are listed at the top of the screen, so you can keep track of the data you have input.

SUMMARY

This chapter provides you with detailed instructions for creating and saving a subroutine library and for using the library with the rest of the programs in this book. This chapter also tells you how to create a library of related programs that can be run from a menu. Each time you need a new program, you add it to the programs you have already saved.

The use of the central subroutine library allows the programs in this book to be very short and easy to enter, and the interactive features built into the programs make them easy to use.

2

HOME AND BUSINESS FINANCE

This chapter contains ten programs useful for many home and business finance applications. For example, let's assume that you are going to deposit money in a bank account for a specific term. One bank pays 8% compounded monthly, and another bank pays 8¼% compounded quarterly. With these programs you can use your computer to find which bank account pays more interest.

You may also wish to contribute regularly to an individual retirement account (IRA). With one of the programs in this chapter you can compute how much money you will have in your IRA at the time you retire. Another program allows you to see if an amount in a savings account is enough for you to retire with.

The last program in this chapter shows you how to put all the other programs together to produce a menu-controlled financial package.

FUTURE VALUE OF A DEPOSIT

Description

Have you ever wondered how quickly a savings account will grow? Would you like to compare the effect of different interest rates and compounding periods?

You can use this program to compute the future value of a deposit. You must specify the amount of the deposit, the number of times per year interest is compounded, the annual interest rate, and the number of years the funds will earn interest. The program assumes a constant interest rate.

Example

Tom deposits $5,000 in a four-year savings account. The bank pays interest at the rate of 12% per annum, compounded quarterly. Tom wishes to know how much his savings will grow in four years. Figure 2.1 shows the results of the computation on the screen. Figure 2.2 is the program listing for the Future Value program.

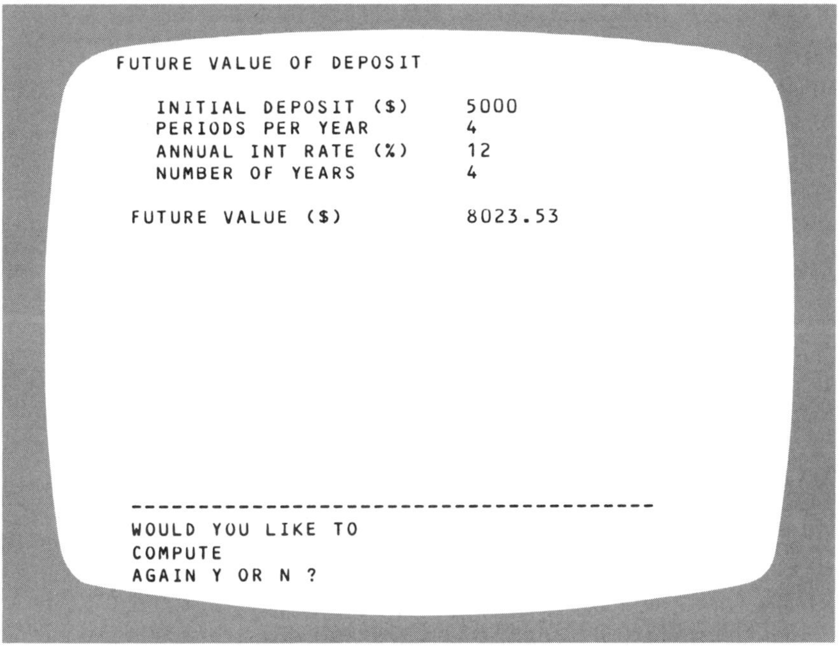

Figure 2.1: Screen Display: Future Value of a Deposit

```
290 REM -------------------------------
300 N$=   "FUTURE VALUE OF DEPOSIT"
310 REM -------------------------------
320 GOSUB 6200: K=1: REM INITIALIZE
330 REM ASK FOR PARAMETERS
340 Q1$="ENTER DATA":Q2$=""
350 Q3$="INITIAL DEPOSIT ($)":GOSUB 6600
360 Q3$="PERIODS PER YEAR":GOSUB 6600
370 Q3$="ANNUAL INT RATE (%)":GOSUB 6600
380 Q3$="NUMBER OF YEARS": GOSUB 6600
390 REM DO THE COMPUTATION
400 PRINT
410 PRINT "FUTURE VALUE ($)";TAB(24);
420 A=P(1)
430 FOR I=1 TO P(2)*P(4)
440 A=A+A*P(3)/100/P(2)
450 NEXT I
460 A=INT(A*100+.5)/100
470 PRINT A
480 Q2$="COMPUTE":GOSUB 3400: REM ASK FOR ANOTHER
490 IF YN$="N" THEN END
500 GOTO 290
```

Figure 2.2: Program Listing: Future Value of a Deposit

FUTURE VALUE OF A SERIES OF DEPOSITS

Description

This program calculates the future value of a series of regular deposits. For example, you can determine the future value of an IRA if you make regular annual contributions. You specify the amount of the payment, the number of payments made per year, the annual interest rate your funds earn, and the number of years you will make the payments. The program assumes that the compounding period and number of payments per year are the same, and that the annual interest rate is constant.

Example

Ann plans to deposit $500 in a savings account every month. Interest is earned at 6% per annum and is compounded monthly. How much money will be in her account in four years? Figure 2.3 shows the screen display for this example. The program listing is in Figure 2.4.

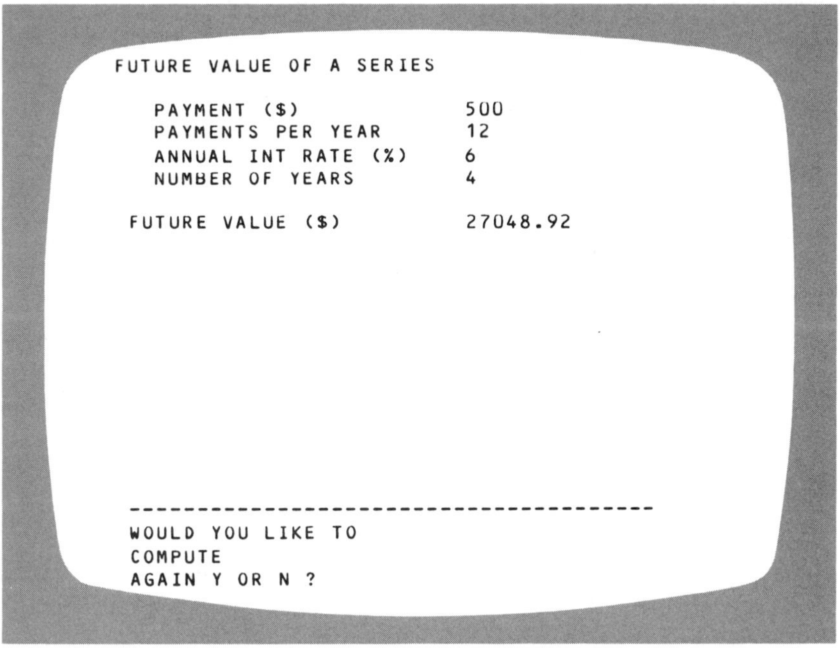

Figure 2.3: Screen Display: Future Value of a Series of Deposits

```
510 REM ------------------------------
520 N$=    "FUTURE VALUE OF A SERIES"
530 REM ------------------------------
540 GOSUB 6200:K=1: REM INITIALIZE
550 REM ASK FOR PARAMETERS
560 Q1$="ENTER DATA":Q2$=""
570 Q3$="PAYMENT ($)":GOSUB6600
580 Q3$="PAYMENTS PER YEAR":GOSUB 6600
590 Q3$="ANNUAL INT RATE (%)":GOSUB 6600
600 Q3$="NUMBER OF YEARS":GOSUB 6600
610 REM COMPUTE RESULT
620 PRINT:PRINT"FUTURE VALUE ($)";TAB(24);
630 A=0
640 FOR I=1 TO P(2)*P(4)
650 A=P(1)+A+A*P(3)/100/P(2)
660 NEXT I
670 A=INT(A*100+.5)/100
680 PRINT A
690 Q2$="COMPUTE":GOSUB 3400: REM ASK FOR ANOTHER
700 IF YN$="N" THEN END
710 GOTO 510
```

Figure 2.4: Program Listing: Future Value of a Series of Deposits

PRESENT VALUE OF AN AMOUNT

Description

Assume that Bob owes you $5,000 in three years. He offers to pay you $4,000 today, and you want to know whether to accept his offer. The Present Value program uses an interest rate you specify to find the present value of a future amount. You should accept Bob's offer if the present value is less than $4,000.

To use this program you supply the future value, the annual interest rate at which your funds earn money, the number of compounding periods per year, and the number of years in the future that the value of the amount is known.

Example

Bill has a note for which he will receive $10,000 five years from now. Bill normally earns 10% interest on his funds, with interest being compounded quarterly. Bill would like to know the present value of his note. Figure 2.5 shows the screen display for the Present Value program; Figure 2.6 lists the Present Value program.

```
PRESENT VALUE OF AMOUNT

   FUTURE VALUE ($)        10000
   PERIODS PER YEAR        4
   ANNUAL INT RATE (%)     10
   NUMBER OF YEARS         5

 PRESENT VALUE ($)         6102.71




 -------------------------------------
 WOULD YOU LIKE TO
 COMPUTE
 AGAIN Y OR N ?
```

Figure 2.5: Screen Display: Present Value of an Amount

```
720 REM ------------------------------
730 N$=   "PRESENT VALUE OF AMOUNT"
740 REM ------------------------------
750 GOSUB 6200: K=1: REM INITIALIZE
760 REM ASK FOR PARMETERS
770 Q1$="ENTER DATA":Q2$=""
780 Q3$="FUTURE VALUE ($)":GOSUB 6600
790 Q3$="PERIODS PER YEAR":GOSUB 6600
800 Q3$="ANNUAL INT RATE (%)":GOSUB 6600
810 Q3$="NUMBER OF YEARS":GOSUB 6600
820 REM DO THE COMPUTATION
830 PRINT:PRINT"PRESENT VALUE ($)";TAB(24);
840 A=P(1)/(1+P(3)/100/P(2))^(P(2)*P(4))
850 A=INT(A*100+.5)/100
860 PRINT A
870 Q2$="COMPUTE":GOSUB 3400: REM ASK FOR ANOTHER
880 IF YN$="N" THEN END
890 GOTO 720
```

Figure 2.6: Program Listing: Present Value of an Amount

PRESENT VALUE OF A SERIES OF PAYMENTS

Description

The previous example shows you how to find the present value of a future amount. With this program you can find the present value of a series of payments. For example, assume that Sally buys your car and pays you $50 a month for three years. After one year she offers you $900 in cash, and you want to know whether to accept her offer. You can use this program to find the answer to your question. You should accept if the present value is less than $900.

To use this program you specify the amount of the payment, the number of payments you receive per year, the number of years for which the payments will continue, and the annual interest rate at which your funds earn interest. We assume that the number of payments per year and the number of compounding periods are identical.

Example

Jackie receives $400 per month in payments. She can earn 10% interest on invested funds, and she wants to know the present value of the payments. The payments will continue for ten years. Figure 2.7 shows the screen display for this example, and Figure 2.8 is the complete program listing.

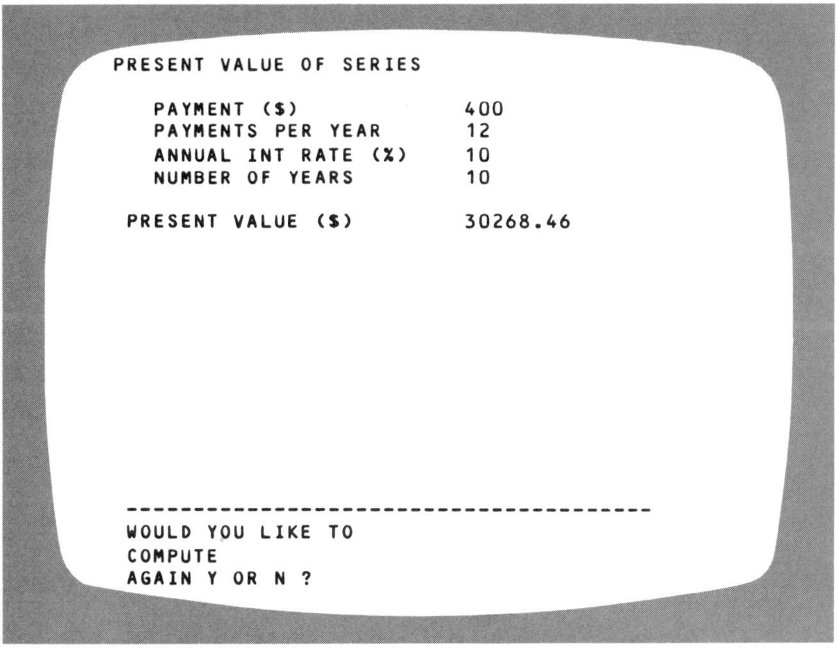

Figure 2.7: Screen Display: Present Value of a Series of Payments

```
900 REM ------------------------------
910 N$=   "PRESENT VALUE OF SERIES"
920 REM ------------------------------
930 GOSUB 6200: K=1: REM INITIALIZE
940 REM ASK FOR PARAMETERS
945 Q1$="ENTER DATA":Q2$=""
950 Q3$="PAYMENT ($)":GOSUB 6600
960 Q3$="PAYMENTS PER YEAR":GOSUB 6600
970 Q3$="ANNUAL INT RATE (%)":GOSUB 6600
980 Q3$="NUMBER OF YEARS":GOSUB 6600
990 REM DO THE COMPUTATION
1000 PRINT: PRINT"PRESENT VALUE ($)";TAB(24);
1010 A=0
1020 FOR I=1 TO P(2)*P(4)
1030 A=A+P(1)/((1+P(3)/100/P(2))^I)
1040 NEXT I
1050 A=INT(A*100+.5)/100
1060 PRINT A
1070 Q2$="COMPUTE": GOSUB 3400: REM ASK FOR ANOTHER
1080 IF YN$="N" THEN END
1090 GOTO 900
```

Figure 2.8: Program Listing: Present Value of a Series of Payments

PAYMENT REQUIRED FOR FUTURE SUM

Description

This program allows you to determine the regular payment necessary to produce a required amount of money in the future. For example, you can use this program to calculate what regular payments will be necessary to take a special vacation, replace a piece of equipment, or save for a college education. You must specify the future sum, the number of payments per year, the annual interest rate at which your funds earn interest, and the number of years to the time you need the money. The program assumes that the number of payments and the compounding periods are identical.

Example

Bob plans to make monthly payments into a college fund for his daughter. He will make the payments for 18 years, and he estimates that he will need $40,000. He can earn 8.5% interest on his college savings account. We show the screen display for this example in Figure 2.9 and the program listing in Figure 2.10.

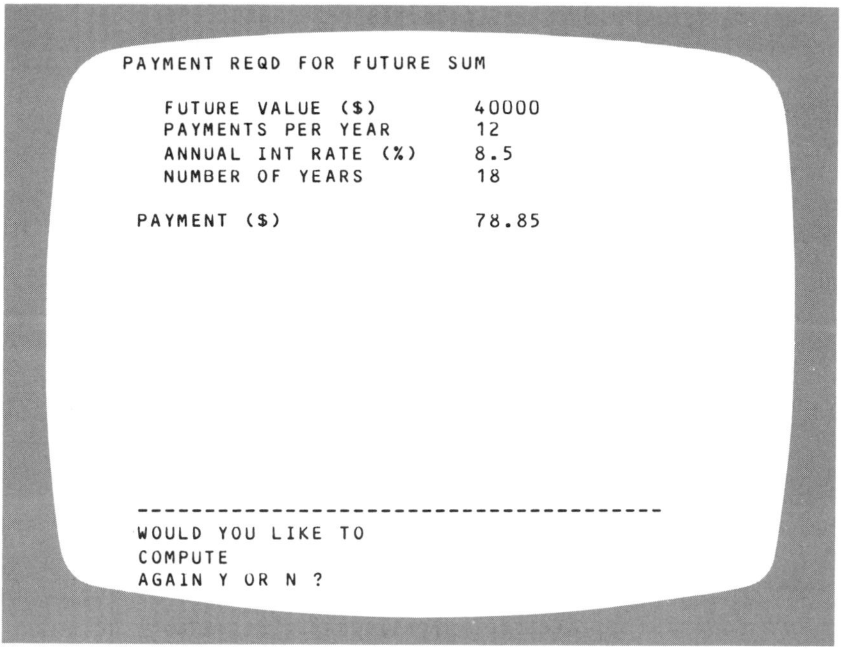

Figure 2.9: Screen Display: Payment Required for Future Sum

```
1100 REM ------------------------------
1110 N$= "PAYMENT REQD FOR FUTURE SUM"
1120 REM ------------------------------
1130 GOSUB 6200: K=1: REM INITIALIZE
1140 REM ASK FOR PARAMETERS
1150 Q1$="ENTER DATA":Q2$=""
1160 Q3$="FUTURE VALUE ($)":GOSUB 6600
1170 Q3$="PAYMENTS PER YEAR":GOSUB 6600
1180 Q3$="ANNUAL INT RATE (%)":GOSUB 6600
1190 Q3$="NUMBER OF YEARS":GOSUB 6600
1200 REM DO THE COMPUTATION
1210 PRINT: PRINT"PAYMENT ($)";TAB(24);
1220 I=P(3)/100/P(2)
1230 Q=P(2)*P(4)
1240 A=P(1)*I/((1+I)^Q-1)
1250 A=INT(A*100+.5)/100
1260 PRINT A
1270 Q2$="COMPUTE":GOSUB 3400: REM ASK FOR ANOTHER
1280 IF YN$="N" THEN END
1290 GOTO 1100
```

Figure 2.10: Program Listing: Payment Required for Future Sum

WITHDRAWAL OF FUNDS

Description

You can use this program to determine how long you can make withdrawals from a bank account before the account runs out of funds. You must specify the initial deposit, the number of withdrawals per year, the interest rate at which the remaining funds earn interest, and the amount of the withdrawal. Again, the program assumes that the number of withdrawals per year and the number of compounding periods are identical.

If the withdrawal amount is less than the interest earned, your bank account will grow rather than run out of funds. The program then displays the message BANK BALANCE IS GROWING. Don't be concerned if this program takes a long time to finish running; the program executes as many times as necessary to find a zero bank balance.

Example

Jack and Jill Jones are ready to retire. They have $200,000 in their bank account, and the account earns 9% interest. Jack and Jill plan to live on $1,600 per month. How long will they be able to withdraw money? Figure 2.11 shows the screen display for this example; the program is listed in Figure 2.12.

```
1300 REM ----------------------------
1310 N$=      "WITHDRAWAL OF FUNDS"
1320 REM ----------------------------
1330 GOSUB 6200: K=1: REM INITIALIZE
1340 REM ASK FOR PARAMETERS
```

Figure 2.12: Program Listing: Withdrawal of Funds (continues)

```
WITHDRAWAL OF FUNDS

   INITIAL DEPOSIT ($)       200000
   WITHDWLS PER YEAR         12
   ANNUAL INT RATE (%)       9
   PAYMENT ($)               1600

 PAYMENTS                    371
 YEARS OF PAYMENTS           30.92










 ---------------------------------------
 WOULD YOU LIKE TO
 COMPUTE
 AGAIN Y OR N ?
```

Figure 2.11: Screen Display: Withdrawal of Funds

```
1350 Q1$="ENTER DATA":Q2$=""
1360 Q3$="INITIAL DEPOSIT ($)":GOSUB 6600
1370 Q3$="WITHDWLS PER YEAR":GOSUB 6600
1380 Q3$="ANNUAL INT RATE (%)":GOSUB 6600
1390 Q3$="PAYMENT ($)":GOSUB 6600
1400 REM DO THE COMPUTATION
1410 PRINT:PRINT"PAYMENTS";TAB(24);
1420 A=P(1):N=1
1430 A=A+A*P(3)/100/P(2)-P(4)
1440 IF A<P(1) THEN 1470
1450 PRINT:PRINT"BANK BALANCE IS GROWING"
1460 GOTO 1530
1470 IF A<P(4) THEN 1500
1480 N=N+1
1490 GOTO 1430
1500 M=INT(N*100+.5)/100: PRINT M
1510 Y=N/12: Y=INT(Y*100+.5)/100
1520 PRINT"YEARS OF PAYMENTS";TAB(24);Y
1530 Q2$="COMPUTE":GOSUB 3400
1540 IF YN$="N" THEN END
1550 GOTO 1300
```

Figure 2.12: Program Listing: Withdrawal of Funds

INTEREST RATE EARNED

Description

The program in this example is useful when you want to determine the interest rate you earn when you know the beginning and ending values of your investment. For example, you can find the equivalent interest rate on the profit from a house sale. To use this program you specify the beginning and ending values of your funds, the number of compounding periods per year, and the number of years over which your funds have grown.

Example

Auntie Mame gave $5,000 to her broker to invest four years ago. She has just received $9,000 in return. She wishes to compute the equivalent interest rate she has earned, with interest compounded quarterly. Figures 2.13 and 2.14 show the screen display and program listing for this example.

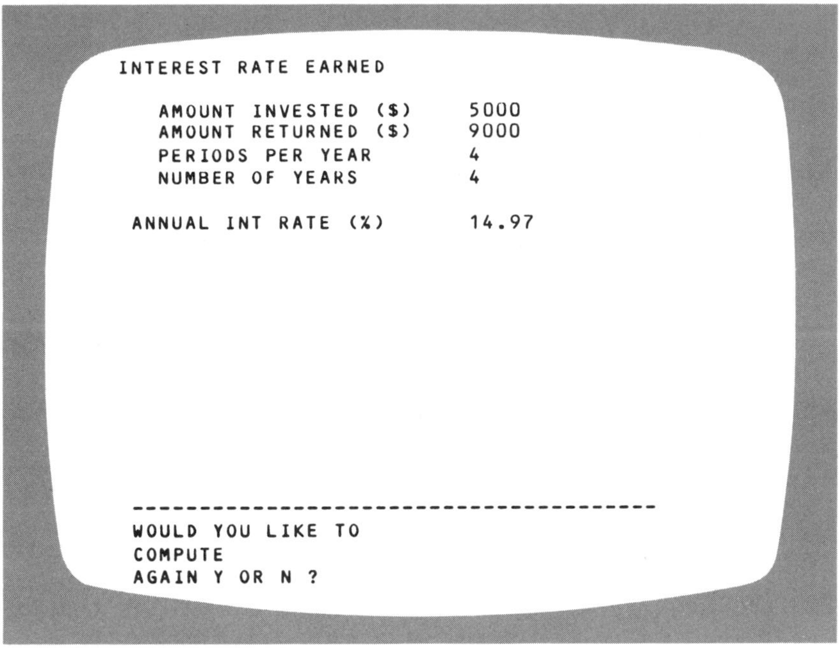

Figure 2.13: Screen Display: Interest Rate Earned

```
1560 REM ----------------------------
1570 N$=      "INTEREST RATE EARNED"
1580 REM ----------------------------
1590 GOSUB 6200: K=1: REM INITIALIZE
1600 REM ASK FOR PARAMETERS
1610 Q1$="ENTER DATA":Q2$=""
1620 Q3$="AMOUNT INVESTED ($)":GOSUB 6600
1630 Q3$="AMOUNT RETURNED ($)":GOSUB 6600
1640 Q3$="PERIODS PER YEAR":GOSUB 6600
1650 Q3$="NUMBER OF YEARS":GOSUB 6600
1660 REM DO THE COMPUTATION
1670 PRINT:PRINT"ANNUAL INT RATE (%)";TAB(24);
1680 Q=P(3)*P(4)
1690 I=((P(2)/P(1))^(1/Q)-1)*100*P(3)
1700 I=INT(I*100+.5)/100
1710 PRINT I
1720 Q2$="COMPUTE":GOSUB 3400
1730 IF YN$="N" THEN END
1740 GOTO 1560
```

Figure 2.14: Program Listing: Interest Rate Earned

NET PRESENT VALUE, UNEVEN CASH FLOWS

Description

Net present value (NPV) analysis is used by financial analysts to determine whether an investment is worthwhile. For an interest rate you specify, a positive NPV indicates that the investment is desirable.

This program is useful when you wish to determine the present value of a series of cash flows. The cash flows need not be the same in every year. You use this program by entering the initial investment you make and the annual interest rate at which your funds earn interest. The program then prompts you for each cash flow. You enter these cash flows as positive or negative numbers, depending on whether you receive or distribute funds. You signal the end of cash flow entries by typing 0.

Example

Tina can buy a note for $5,000. She will receive annual payments of $500, $1,500, $1,500, $1,500, and $1,000. Tina would like her funds to earn 12% annual interest. What is the net present value of her investment? The display in Figure 2.15 is negative, indicating that she is not earning 12%; thus she should not buy the note. A complete program listing is shown in Figure 2.16.

```
1750 REM ------------------------------
1760 N$=    "NPV, UNEVEN CASH FLOWS"
1770 REM ------------------------------
1780 GOSUB 6200: K=1: REM INITIALIZE
1790 REM ASK FOR PARAMETERS
1800 Q1$="ENTER DATA":Q2$=""
```

Figure 2.16: Program Listing: Net Present Value, Uneven Cash Flows (continues)

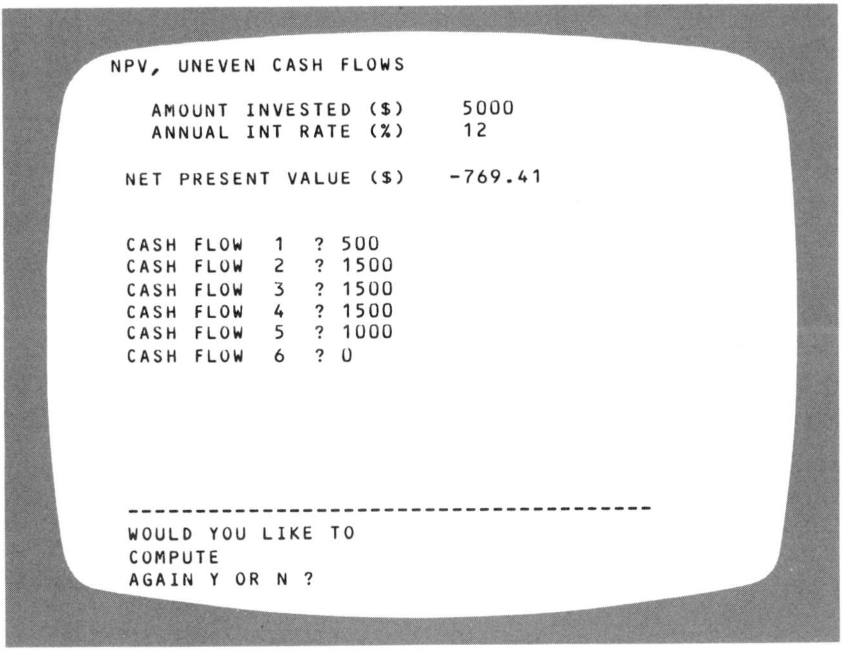

Figure 2.15: Screen Display: Net Present Value, Uneven Cash Flows

```
1810 Q3$="AMOUNT INVESTED ($)":GOSUB 6600
1820 Q3$="ANNUAL INT RATE (%)":GOSUB 6600
1830 Q1$="ENTER ANNUAL CASH FLOWS"
1840 Q2$="IN ORDER RECEIVED"
1850 Q3$="TYPE 0 WHEN DONE"
1860 GOSUB 5000: REM CALL DIALOG
1870 N=0:NPV=-P(1)
1880 N=N+1: Y=N-INT((N-1)/10)*10+8
1890 X=1:GOSUB 4200: REM LOCATE
1900 PRINT S$:GOSUB 4200
1910 PRINT"CASH FLOW ";N;TAB(14);
1920 INPUT I: IF I=0 THEN 1950
1930 NPV=NPV+I/(1+P(2)/100)^N
1940 GOTO 1880
1950 X=1: Y=6:GOSUB 4200: REM LOCATE
1960 PRINT"NET PRESENT VALUE ($)";TAB(24);
1970 A=INT(NPV*100+.5)/100
1980 PRINT A
1990 Q2$="COMPUTE":GOSUB 3400
2000 IF YN$="N" THEN END
2010 GOTO 1750
```

Figure 2.16: Program Listing: Net Present Value, Uneven Cash Flows

TIME TO DOUBLE

Description

This program computes the time it will take for the funds you invest to double. To use the program you enter the annual interest rate and number of compounding periods per year.

Example

Fred's bank compounds interest four times yearly and pays 12% interest per annum. How many years will it take Fred to double a $5,000 investment? We display the results of this program in Figure 2.17; a program listing is shown in Figure 2.18.

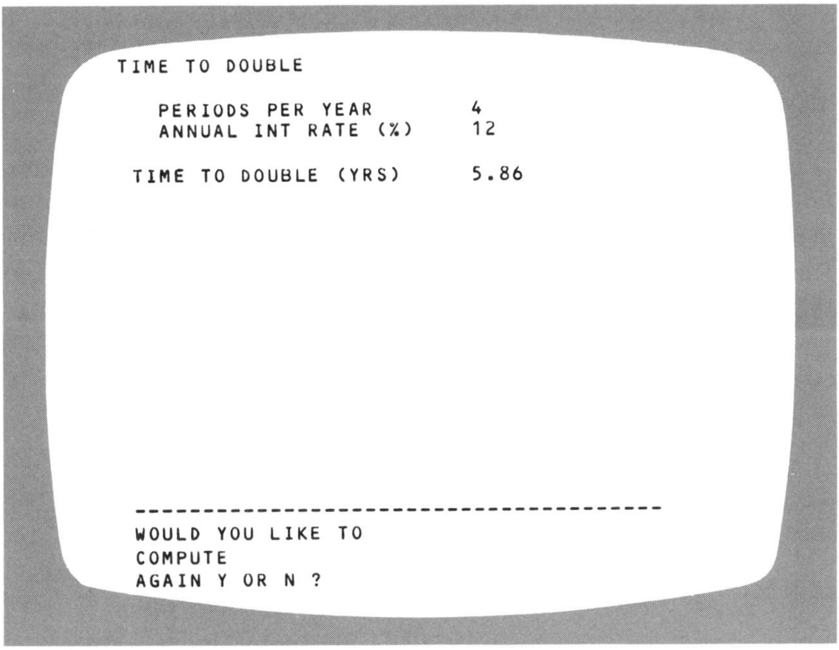

Figure 2.17: Screen Display: Time to Double

```
2020 REM ----------------------------
2030 N$=        "TIME TO DOUBLE"
2040 REM ----------------------------
2050 GOSUB 6200: K=1: REM INITIALIZE
2060 REM ASK FOR PARAMETERS
2070 Q1$="ENTER DATA":Q2$=""
2080 Q3$="PERIODS PER YEAR":GOSUB 6600
2090 Q3$="ANNUAL INT RATE (%)": GOSUB 6600
2100 REM DO THE COMPUTATION
2110 PRINT:PRINT"TIME TO DOUBLE (YRS)";TAB(24);
2120 I=P(2)/100/P(1)
2130 Y=LOG(2)/(P(1)*LOG(1+I))
2140 Y=INT(Y*100+.5)/100
2150 PRINT Y
2160 Q2$="COMPUTE":GOSUB 3400
2170 IF YN$="N" THEN END
2180 GOTO 2020
```

Figure 2.18: Program Listing: Time to Double

EQUIVALENT INTEREST RATE

Description

Many of the programs in this chapter assume that the number of compounding periods and the number of payments are identical. This program allows you to determine an equivalent interest rate when the two periods are not the same. To use the program, enter the annual interest rate, the number of compounding periods, and the number of payments you want to make per year (desired periods). The program then computes an equivalent interest rate that you can use.

Example

You make deposits monthly into an account, and you wish to determine the future value of the deposits. The interest on this account is 12% per annum, compounded quarterly. As shown in Figure 2.19, the equivalent interest rate is 11.88%. You should use this figure and then run the Future Value of a Series of Deposits program to compute your final answer. The program listing for this example is given in Figure 2.20.

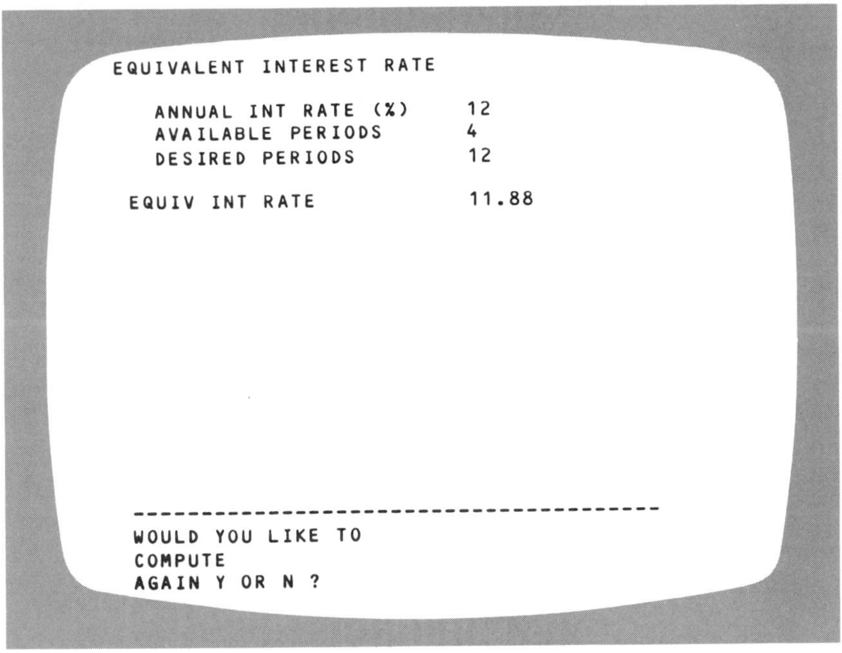

Figure 2.19: Screen Display: Equivalent Interest Rate

```
2190 REM ------------------------------
2200 N$=   "EQUIVALENT INTEREST RATE"
2210 REM ------------------------------
2220 GOSUB 6200: K=1: REM INITIALIZE
2230 REM ASK FOR PARAMETERS
2240 Q1$="ENTER DATA":Q2$=""
2250 Q3$="ANNUAL INT RATE (%)":GOSUB 6600
2260 Q3$="AVAILABLE PERIODS":GOSUB 6600
2270 Q3$="DESIRED PERIODS":GOSUB 6600
2280 I=P(1):Q2=P(2):Q1=P(3)
2290 IEQ=Q1*(1+I/100/Q2)^(Q2/Q1)-Q1
2300 PRINT:PRINT"EQUIV INT RATE";TAB(24);
2310 IEQ=INT(IEQ*10000+.5)/100
2320 PRINT IEQ
2330 Q2$="COMPUTE":GOSUB 3400
2340 IF YN$="N" THEN END
2350 GOTO 2190
```

Figure 2.20: Program Listing: Equivalent Interest Rate

FINANCIAL PROGRAMS MENU

All of the programs in this chapter have been entered with distinct program line numbers. If you save all the programs together in one diskette or tape file, you can use the menu program we develop here to run any of these programs. The menu is set up so that you press a single key to select the program you want to run.

Remember, when these programs are used with the menu, you must replace the END instruction at the end of every program with a RETURN instruction. You should enter the menu program by first loading your financial programs, then keying in the menu program. Then save the programs and menu with the SAVE command. The menu is shown in Figure 2.21. Figure 2.22 shows the menu selection program.

After you have run the financial programs you need, you can return to BASIC by pressing the reset key—the cursor will appear on a blank line, and you can then load another set of programs.

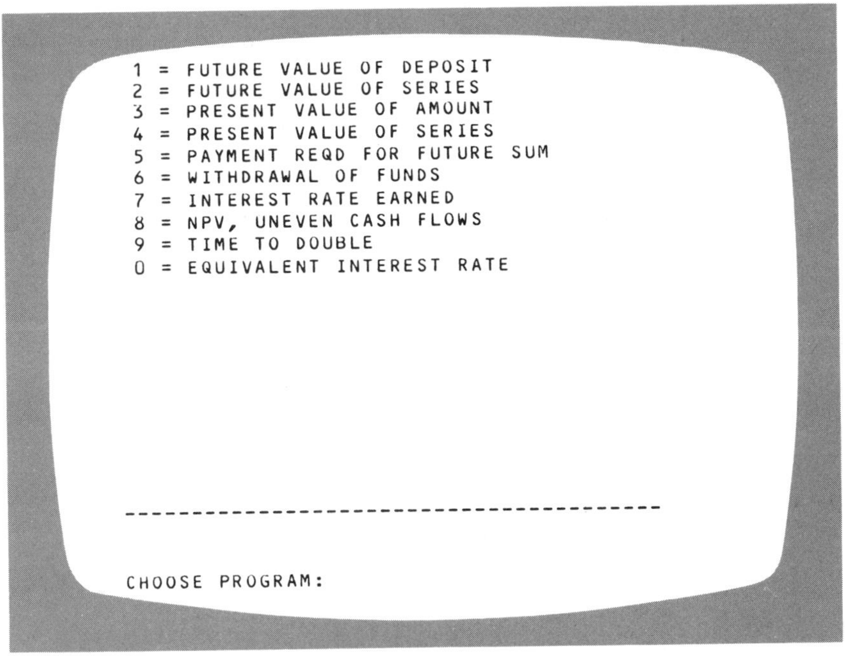

Figure 2.21: Screen Display: Financial Programs Menu

```
100 REM ------------------------------
110 N$=     "FINANCIAL PROGRAMS"
120 REM ------------------------------
130 GOSUB 6200: REM INITIALIZE
140 REM SET UP MENU ARRAY
150 X$(1)="FUTURE VALUE OF DEPOSIT"
160 X$(2)="FUTURE VALUE OF SERIES"
170 X$(3)="PRESENT VALUE OF AMOUNT"
180 X$(4)="PRESENT VALUE OF SERIES"
190 X$(5)="PAYMENT REQD FOR FUTURE SUM"
200 X$(6)="WITHDRAWAL OF FUNDS"
210 X$(7)="INTEREST RATE EARNED"
220 X$(8)="NPV, UNEVEN CASH FLOWS"
230 X$(9)="TIME TO DOUBLE"
240 X$(10)="EQUIVALENT INTEREST RATE"
250 N=10: GOSUB 7000: REM DISPLAY MENU
260 REM SELECT PROGRAM
270 ON X GOSUB 290,510,720,900,1100,1300,1560,1750,2020,2190
280 GOTO 100
```

Figure 2.22: Program Listing: Financial Programs Menu

3

USEFUL BUSINESS PROGRAMS

This chapter presents ten helpful business programs. These programs enable you to prepare depreciation schedules, find the economic ordering quantity, and solve many other business problems.

For example, you may be starting a business or running a charity event; the Break-Even Point program will calculate how many items or tickets you must sell to produce a profit. Whether you are a salesperson or employ a salesperson, the Salesperson's Commission program allows you to find the commission due for a given sales volume. The Wages with Overtime program makes it simple to calculate the salary due when overtime is worked. This program adds base pay and overtime pay to find the total salary due. We also provide an executive decision making program, which can be used when all else fails.

STRAIGHT-LINE DEPRECIATION

Description

This program computes a yearly depreciation schedule based on the straight-line method. To depreciate an asset, you specify the present book value, the estimated salvage value, and the life of the asset in years. If your asset has a life longer than ten years, the program displays the schedule for the first ten years and then pauses. When you are ready to review years 11–20, you simply press any key, and the schedule for those years is displayed.

Example

Let's set up a depreciation schedule for an office copier. We presently value the copier at $5,000. We expect to use the copier for six years and then sell it for $1,000. Figure 3.1 shows the screen display of the depreciation schedule. Figure 3.2 is a listing of the depreciation program.

```
280 REM ------------------------------
290 N$=  "STRAIGHT-LINE DEPRECIATION"
300 REM ------------------------------
310 GOSUB 6200: K=1
```

Figure 3.2: Program Listing: Straight-Line Depreciation (continues)

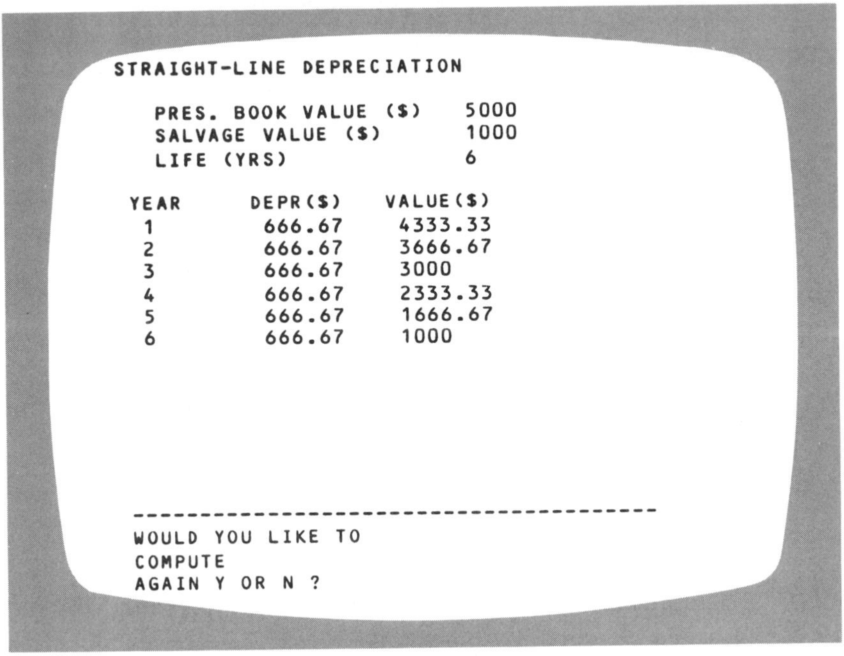

Figure 3.1: Screen Display: Straight-Line Depreciation

```
320 REM GET INPUT PARAMETERS
330 Q1$="ENTER DATA":Q2$=""
340 Q3$="PRES. BOOK VALUE ($)":GOSUB 6600
350 Q3$="SALVAGE VALUE ($)":GOSUB 6600
360 Q3$="LIFE (YRS)":GOSUB 6600
370 REM PRINT DEPRECIATION SCHEDULE
380 D=(P(1)-P(2))/P(3)
390 PRINT
400 PRINT"YEAR      DEPR($)    VALUE($)"
410 FOR I=1 TO P(3)
415 Y=I-INT((I-1)/10)*10+7:X=1
416 GOSUB 4200: PRINT S$: GOSUB 4200
420 PRINT I;TAB(9);
430 D1=INT(D*100+.5)/100:D2=INT((P(1)-D*I)*100+.5)/100
440 PRINT D1;TAB(19);D2
450 IF I/10=INT(I/10) THEN GOSUB 7400
460 NEXT I
470 Q2$="COMPUTE":GOSUB 3400: REM ASK FOR ANOTHER
480 IF YN$="N" THEN END
490 GOTO 280
```

Figure 3.2: Program Listing: Straight-Line Depreciation

DECLINING-BALANCE DEPRECIATION

Description

This program makes it easy to calculate depreciation schedules based on the declining-balance method, which is an accelerated method of depreciation. Accelerated depreciation methods are often used to provide more favorable tax treatment than the straight-line method provides. The declining-balance method multiplies the remaining book value of an asset by an acceleration factor and then divides by the life of the asset in years. You must specify the initial book value of the asset, its useful life, and the acceleration factor. Typical acceleration factors are 150%, 175%, and 200%; the declining-balance method ignores the salvage value.

Example

Let's now depreciate the office copier in the previous example by the declining-balance method. In this example we use an acceleration factor of 150%. The depreciation schedule appears in Figure 3.3 and the program listing in Figure 3.4.

```
500 REM-------------------------------
510 N$="DECLINING-BALANCE DEPRECIATION"
520 REM-------------------------------
530 GOSUB 6200: K=1
```

Figure 3.4: Program Listing: Declining-Balance Depreciation (continues)

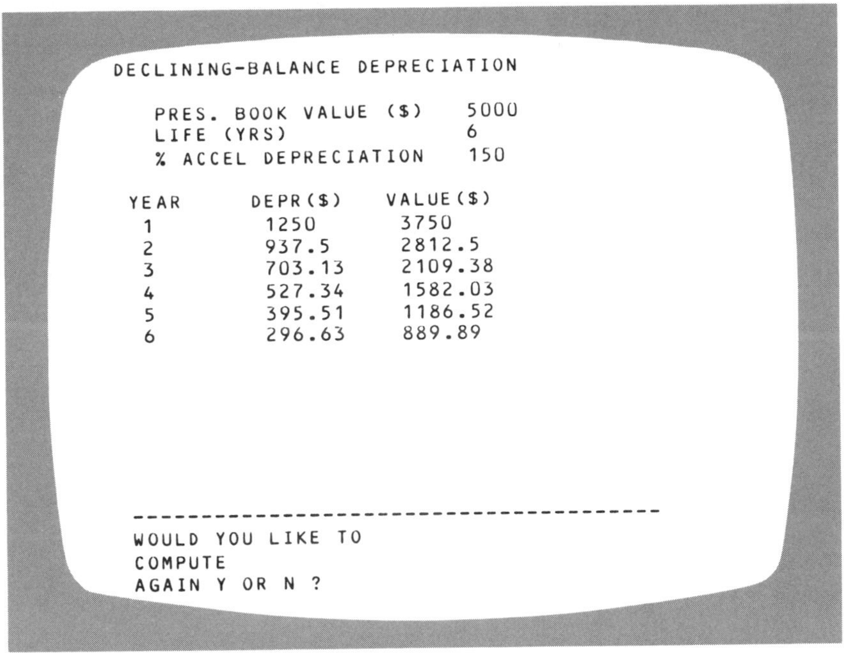

Figure 3.3: Screen Display: Declining-Balance Depreciation

```
540 REM GET INPUT PARAMETERS
550 Q1$="ENTER DATA":Q2$=""
560 Q3$="PRES. BOOK VALUE ($)":GOSUB 6600
570 Q3$="LIFE (YRS)":GOSUB 6600
580 Q3$="% ACCEL DEPRECIATION":GOSUB 6600
590 REM PRINT DEPREC SCHEDULE
600 RV=P(1)
610 PRINT
620 PRINT"YEAR      DEPR($)    VALUE($)"
630 FOR I=1 TO P(2)
640 Y=I-INT((I-1)/10)*10+7:X=1
650 GOSUB 4200:PRINT S$: GOSUB 4200
660 D=RV*P(3)/100/P(2):RV=RV-D
670 D1=INT(D*100+.5)/100:D2=INT(RV*100+.5)/100
680 PRINT I;TAB(9);D1;TAB(19);D2
690 IF I/10=INT(I/10) THEN GOSUB 7400
700 NEXT I
710 Q2$="COMPUTE":GOSUB 3400
720 IF YN$="N" THEN END
730 GOTO 500
```

Figure 3.4: Program Listing: Declining-Balance Depreciation

SUM-OF-YEARS'-DIGITS DEPRECIATION

Description

We now show a second method of accelerated depreciation, the sum of the years' digits. This depreciation method multiplies the remaining book value by the ratio of the number of remaining years to the sum of the years of life. If the life of the asset is five years, the sum of the years of life is

$$5 + 4 + 3 + 2 + 1 = 15$$

You again specify the present book value, salvage value, and life of the asset. Your computer simplifies this otherwise tedious calculation.

Example

Let us produce a sum-of-the-years'-digits depreciation schedule for the office copier in the prior examples. The schedule is shown in Figure 3.5; the program listing appears in Figure 3.6.

```
740 REM-----------------------------------
750 N$="SUM-OF-YEARS'-DIGITS DEPRECIATION"
760 REM-----------------------------------
770 GOSUB 6200: K=1
780 REM GET INPUT PARAMETERS
```

Figure 3.6: Program Listing: Sum-of-Years'-Digits Depreciation (continues)

```
SUM-OF-YEARS'-DIGITS DEPRECIATION

   PRES. BOOK VALUE ($)    5000
   SALVAGE VALUE ($)       1000
   LIFE (YRS)              6

 YEAR      DEPR($)    VALUE($)
  1         1142.86    3857.14
  2         952.38     2904.76
  3         761.9      2142.86
  4         571.43     1571.43
  5         380.95     1190.48
  6         190.48     1000

 --------------------------------------
 WOULD YOU LIKE TO
 COMPUTE
 AGAIN Y OR N ?
```

Figure 3.5: Screen Display: Sum-of-Years'-Digits Depreciation

```
790 Q1$="ENTER DATA":Q2$=""
800 Q3$="PRES. BOOK VALUE ($)":GOSUB6600
810 Q3$="SALVAGE VALUE ($)":GOSUB 6600
820 Q3$="LIFE (YRS)":GOSUB 6600
830 REM PRINT DEPR SCHEDULE
840 D=P(1)-P(2)
850 RV=P(1)
860 PRINT
870 PRINT"YEAR      DEPR($)    VALUE($)"
880 FOR I=1 TO P(3)
890 D1=D*(P(3)+1-I)/(P(3)*(P(3)+1)/2)
900 RV=RV-D1
910 D2=INT(D1*100+.5)/100:D3=INT(RV*100+.5)/100
920 Y=I-INT((I-1)/10)*10+7:X=1
930 GOSUB 4200: PRINT S$: GOSUB 4200
940 PRINT I;TAB(9);D2;TAB(19);D3
950 IF I/10=INT(I/10) THEN GOSUB 7400
960 NEXT I
970 Q2$="COMPUTE":GOSUB 3400: REM ASK FOR ANOTHER
980 IF YN$="N" THEN END
990 GOTO 740
```

Figure 3.6: Program Listing: Sum-of-Years'-Digits Depreciation

BREAK-EVEN POINT

Description

This program allows you to find the number of items you must sell for a business or product line to break even. To use this program you must specify the fixed costs of the business (overhead), the cost per unit to manufacture or buy your product, and the sales price per unit.

Example

Harry buys novelty items for $3.00 each and plans to sell them for $6.00 each through mail order. If Harry plans to spend $1,500 to promote and sell the items, how many units must he sell to break even? The screen display for this example is shown in Figure 3.7; the program listing appears in Figure 3.8.

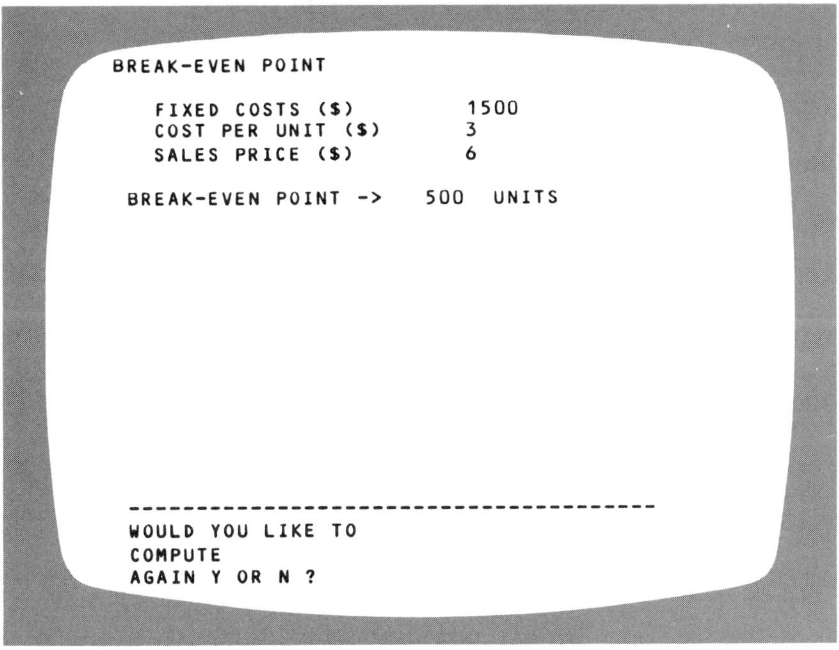

Figure 3.7: Screen Display: Break-Even Point

```
1000 REM ------------------------------
1010 N$=       "BREAK-EVEN POINT"
1020 REM ------------------------------
1030 GOSUB 6200: K=1
1040 REM GET INPUT PARAMETERS
1050 Q1$="ENTER DATA":Q2$=""
1060 Q3$="FIXED COSTS ($)":GOSUB 6600
1070 Q3$="COST PER UNIT ($)":GOSUB 6600
1080 Q3$="SALES PRICE ($)":GOSUB 6600
1090 PRINT
1100 PRINT"BREAK-EVEN POINT ->  ";
1110 US=INT(P(1)/(P(3)-P(2))*100+.5)/100
1120 PRINT US;" UNITS"
1130 Q2$="COMPUTE":GOSUB 3400: REM ASK FOR ANOTHER
1140 IF YN$="N" THEN END
1150 GOTO 1000
```

Figure 3.8: Program Listing: Break-Even Point

ECONOMIC ORDERING QUANTITY

Description

Operations researchers have developed a method to compute the most economic quantity of items for a manufacturer to order. This program does the computation for you. To use this program, specify the cost to place a purchase order, the number of units you use annually, and the annual carrying cost per unit. Carrying cost is defined as the interest rate your funds earn multiplied by the purchase price per item.

Example

Ray is the production manager for a small manufacturing company. He wants to calculate the economic ordering quantity for pumps that are used in the company's products. The company uses 15,000 pumps annually. The annual carrying cost of the pumps is $5 each, and a purchase order costs $75. What is the economic ordering quantity? Figure 3.9 shows the result of Ray's analysis. Figure 3.10 displays the program listing.

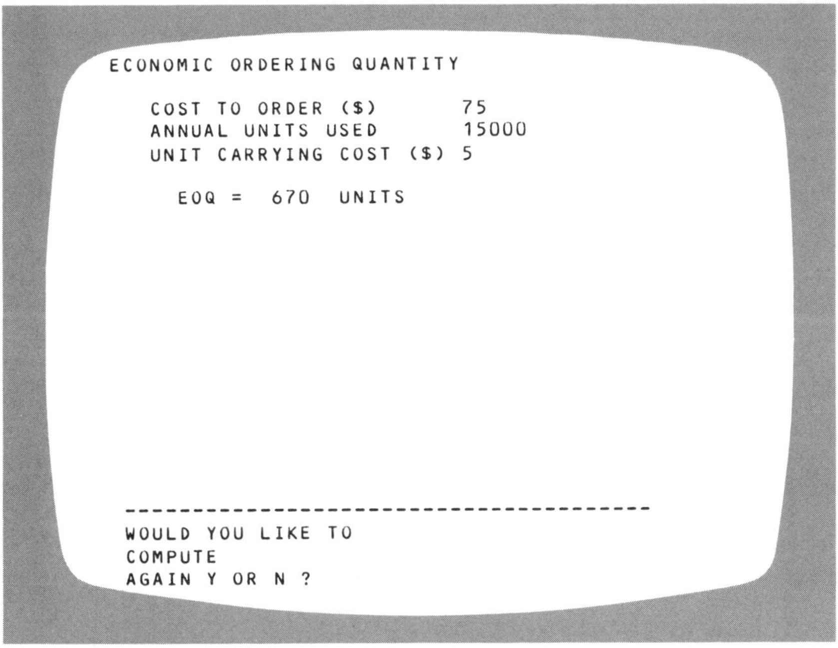

Figure 3.9: Screen Display: Economic Ordering Quantity

```
1160 REM -----------------------------
1170 N$=  "ECONOMIC ORDERING QUANTITY"
1180 REM -----------------------------
1190 GOSUB 6200: K=1
1200 REM GET INPUT PARAMETERS
1210 Q1$="ENTER DATA":Q2$=""
1220 Q3$="COST TO ORDER ($)":GOSUB 6600
1230 Q3$="ANNUAL UNITS USED":GOSUB 6600
1240 Q3$="UNIT CARRYING COST ($)":GOSUB 6600
1250 REM COMPUTE AND PRINT
1260 PRINT
1270 EOQ=INT(SQR(2*P(1)*P(2)/P(3)))
1280 PRINT"    EOQ = ";EOQ;" UNITS"
1290 Q2$="COMPUTE":GOSUB 3400
1300 IF YN$="N" THEN END
1310 GOTO 1160
```

Figure 3.10: Program Listing: Economic Ordering Quantity

SALES PRICE WITH DISCOUNT

Description

Here is a program that enables you to compute the total sales price, with tax, of an item that is selling at a discount. To use this program you specify the retail price, discount percentage, and sales tax rate.

Example

Betty wants to buy a television set that is being sold at a 15% discount. The retail price of the television set is $350 and the sales tax is 6.5%. How much will Betty have to pay? Figure 3.11 shows the screen display for this example. Figure 3.12 shows the listing for the Sales Price with Discount program.

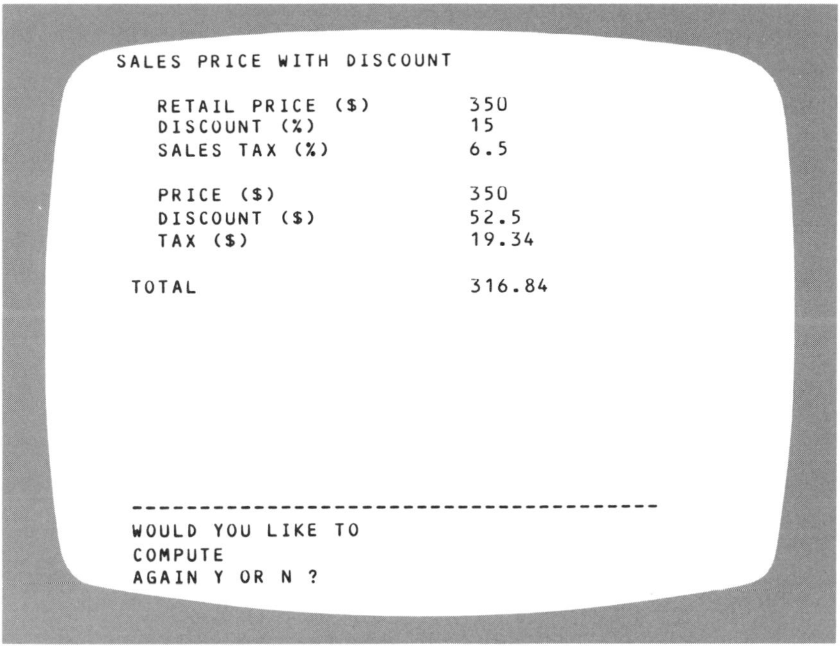

Figure 3.11: Screen Display: Sales Price with Discount

```
1320 REM ------------------------------
1330 N$=  "SALES PRICE WITH DISCOUNT"
1340 REM ------------------------------
1350 GOSUB 6200:K=1
1360 REM GET INPUT PARAMETERS
1370 Q1$="ENTER DATA":Q2$=""
1380 Q3$="RETAIL PRICE ($)":GOSUB 6600
1390 Q3$="DISCOUNT (%)":GOSUB 6600
1400 Q3$="SALES TAX (%)":GOSUB 6600
1410 REM COMPUTE AND PRINT
1420 PRINT
1430 P(1)=INT(P(1)*100+.5)/100
1440 PRINT"  PRICE ($)";TAB(24);P(1)
1450 D=INT(P(1)*P(2)+.5)/100
1460 PRINT"  DISCOUNT ($)";TAB(24);D
1470 T=INT((P(1)-D)*P(3)+.5)/100
1480 PRINT"  TAX ($)";TAB(24);T
1490 PRINT
1500 PRINT"TOTAL";TAB(24);P(1)-D+T
1510 Q2$="COMPUTE":GOSUB 3400
1520 IF YN$="N" THEN END
1530 GOTO 1320
```

Figure 3.12: Program Listing: Sales Price with Discount

WEIGHTED AVERAGE

Description

There are many times when you will need to compute the weighted average of a number of items. Weighted averages can be used to find the average cost of stocks when you buy shares of stock at different times and different values. Weighted averages are also one way of finding the value of a business's inventory when the same item is bought at different prices.

This program rapidly computes the weighted average of a series of quantities. You use the program by entering the cost per unit followed by the number of units purchased for each item. You end the entry process by typing 0 for both the unit value and the number of units.

Example

Lloyd has been buying stock in a rapidly appreciating electronics company. He would like to calculate his average cost of shares; he has purchased four shares at $10 each, four shares at $40 each, and two shares at $60 each. Figures 3.13 and 3.14 show the result of the calculation and the program listing.

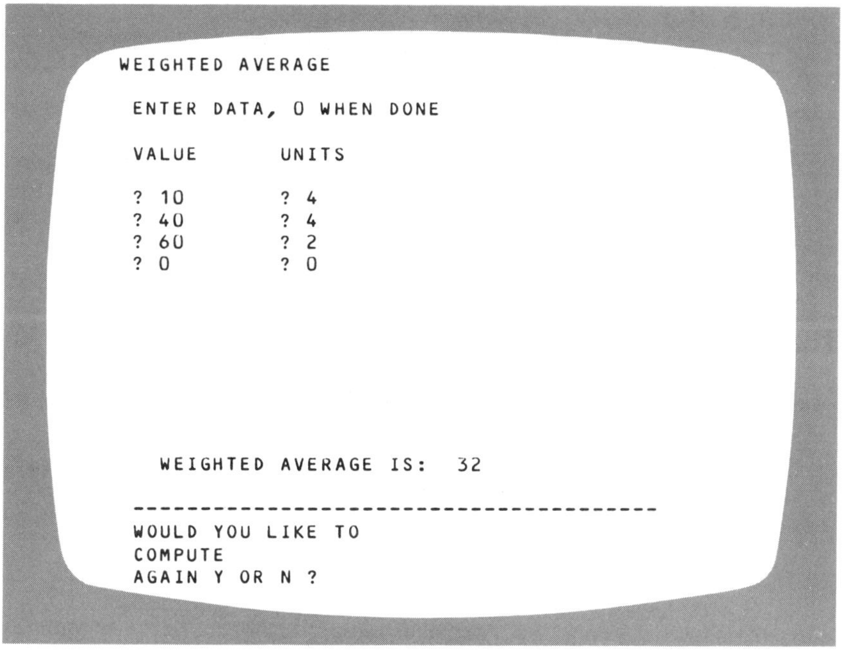

Figure 3.13: Screen Display: Weighted Average

```
1540 REM -----------------------------
1550 N$=      "WEIGHTED AVERAGE"
1560 REM -----------------------------
1570 GOSUB 6200:K=1
1580 REM GET INPUT PARAMETERS
1590 PRINT"ENTER DATA, 0 WHEN DONE"
1600 PRINT: PRINT"VALUE       UNITS"
1610 ND=0:AVE=0:U=0
1620 Y=ND-INT(ND/10)*10+7:X=1
1630 GOSUB 4200: PRINT S$: GOSUB 4200
1640 INPUT D1: X=12: GOSUB 4200: INPUT D2
1650 IF D2=0 THEN 1700
1660 ND=ND+1
1670 AVE=AVE+D1*D2
1680 U=U+D2
1690 GOTO 1620
1700 AVE=INT(AVE/U)
1710 X=3: Y=19:GOSUB 4200
1720 PRINT"WEIGHTED AVERAGE IS: ";AVE
1730 Q2$="COMPUTE":GOSUB 3400:REM ASK FOR ANOTHER
1740 IF YN$="N" THEN END
1750 GOTO 1540
```

Figure 3.14: Program Listing: Weighted Average

SALESPERSON'S COMMISSION

Description

We will now enter a program to calculate the commission due to a salesperson. You specify the salesperson's monthly draw, monthly sales volume, and commission percentage. A negative result indicates that the salesperson has not sold his quota.

Example

Sam Spade receives a monthly draw of $1,200. He earns 6% commission on the sales he makes as a furniture salesman. What commission is he owed in a month during which he sells $25,000 worth of furniture? Figures 3.15 and 3.16 are the screen display and the program listing for the Salesperson's Commission program.

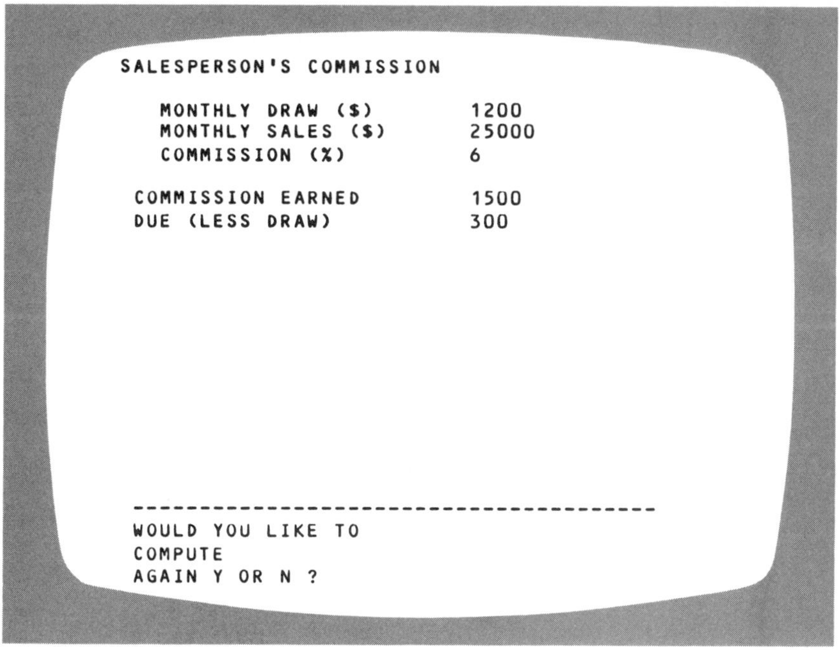

Figure 3.15: Screen Display: Salesperson's Commission

```
1760 REM ------------------------------
1770 N$=  "SALESPERSON'S COMMISSION"
1780 REM ------------------------------
1790 GOSUB 6200: K=1
1800 REM GET INPUT PARAMETERS
1810 Q1$="ENTER DATA":Q2$=""
1820 Q3$="MONTHLY DRAW ($)":GOSUB 6600
1830 Q3$="MONTHLY SALES ($)":GOSUB 6600
1840 Q3$="COMMISSION (%)":GOSUB 6600
1850 REM COMPUTE AND PRINT
1860 PRINT
1870 C=INT(P(2)*P(3)+.5)/100
1880 PRINT"COMMISSION EARNED";TAB(24);C
1890 PRINT"DUE (LESS DRAW)";TAB(24);C-P(1)
1900 Q2$="COMPUTE":GOSUB 3400: REM ASK FOR ANOTHER
1910 IF YN$="N" THEN END
1920 GOTO 1760
```

Figure 3.16: Program Listing: Salesperson's Commission

WAGES WITH OVERTIME

Description

This program makes it easy to calculate the total wages due an employee who earns overtime pay at a premium rate. You enter the employee's base hourly pay, the overtime pay factor, and the number of base and overtime hours that the employee worked.

Example

Toni earns $10.00 an hour as a machine operator. During a very busy week she works her regular 40 hours plus 12 hours at overtime pay. You wish to compute her total wages, with overtime paid at time and a half. Figures 3.17 and 3.18 show the results of the overtime computation and the program listing.

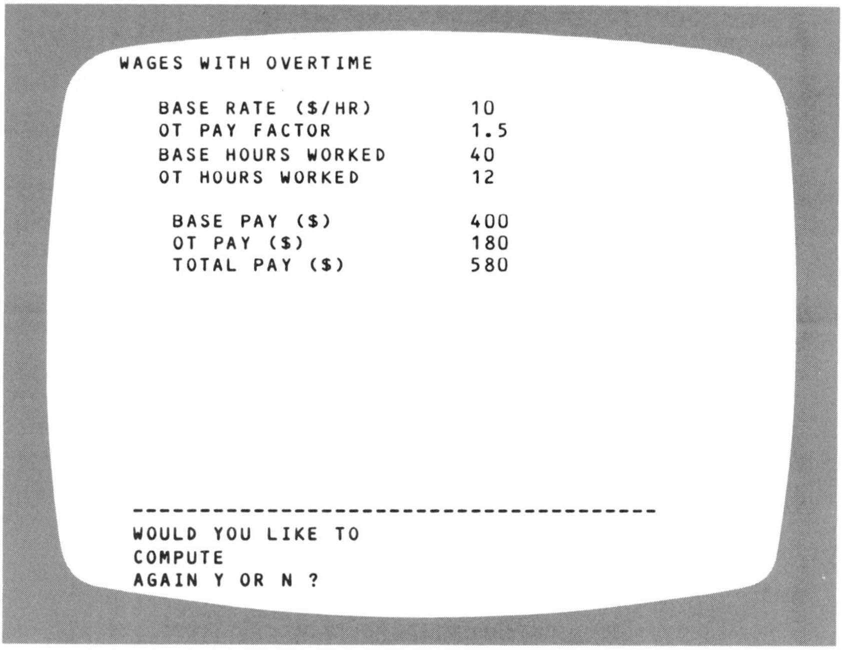

Figure 3.17: Screen Display: Wages with Overtime

```
1930 REM -----------------------------
1940 N$=      "WAGES WITH OVERTIME"
1950 REM -----------------------------
1960 GOSUB 6200: K=1
1970 REM GET INPUT PARAMETERS
1980 Q1$="ENTER DATA":Q2$=""
1990 Q3$="BASE RATE ($/HR)":GOSUB 6600
2000 Q3$="OT PAY FACTOR":GOSUB 6600
2010 Q3$="BASE HOURS WORKED":GOSUB 6600
2020 Q3$="OT HOURS WORKED":GOSUB 6600
2030 REM COMPUTE AND PRINT
2040 PRINT
2050 B=INT(P(1)*P(3)*100+.5)/100
2060 PRINT"   BASE PAY ($)";TAB(24);B
2070 O=INT(P(1)*P(2)*P(4)*100+.5)/100
2080 PRINT"   OT PAY ($)";TAB(24);O
2090 PRINT"   TOTAL PAY ($)";TAB(24);O+B
2100 Q2$="COMPUTE":GOSUB 3400: REM ASK FOR ANOTHER
2110 IF YN$="N" THEN END
2120 GOTO 1930
```

Figure 3.18: Program Listing: Wages with Overtime

EXECUTIVE DECISION MAKER

Description

When all else fails, you can use this program to assist you in making key business decisions. Simply type your question into the computer. The program uses advanced decision theory to answer your question. (This program is fun to run at a cocktail party or other social gatherings.)

Example

Ed needs to know whether a high-risk project will succeed. Because his staff members cannot provide him with a definite recommendation, he asks his computer, as shown in Figure 3.19. The listing for this program is in Figure 3.20.

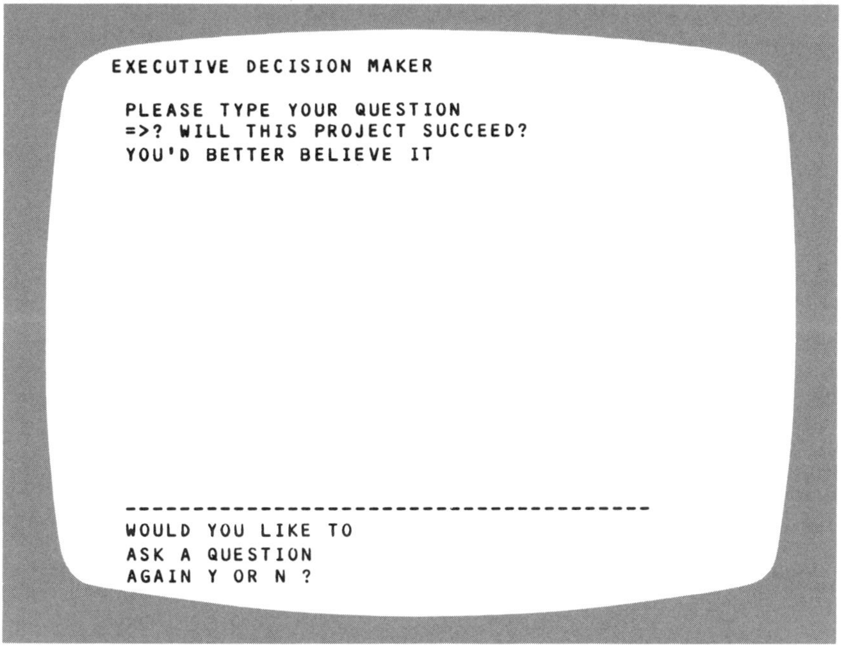

Figure 3.19: Screen Display: Executive Decision Maker

```
2130 REM ------------------------------
2140 N$=  "EXECUTIVE DECISION MAKER"
2150 REM ------------------------------
2160 GOSUB 6200: K=1
2170 PRINT"PLEASE TYPE YOUR QUESTION"
2180 PRINT"=>";
2190 INPUT Q$: Y=LEN(Q$)
2200 IF Y<6 THEN 2220
2210 Y=INT(Y/2):GOTO 2200
2220 ON Y GOTO 2230,2240,2250,2260,2270
2230 PRINT"NOT ON YOUR LIFE":GOTO 2280
2240 PRINT"GO FOR IT!!!":GOTO 2280
2250 PRINT"YOU'D BETTER BELIEVE IT":GOTO 2280
2260 PRINT"FLIP A COIN!":GOTO 2280
2270 PRINT"MAKE YOUR BREAK- QUICKLY"
2280 Q2$="ASK A QUESTION":GOSUB 3400
2290 IF YN$="N" THEN END
2300 GOTO 2130
```

Figure 3.20: Program Listing: Executive Decision Maker

BUSINESS PROGRAMS MENU

If you save all the programs in this chapter in one diskette or tape file, you can add the menu program shown here to run the other programs. You select the programs by using the number keys of your computer. Remember to replace the END instruction in each program with a RETURN command. Review the menu entry instructions in Chapter 2 prior to creating your menu. Figures 3.21 and 3.22 display an image of the menu and the menu selection program.

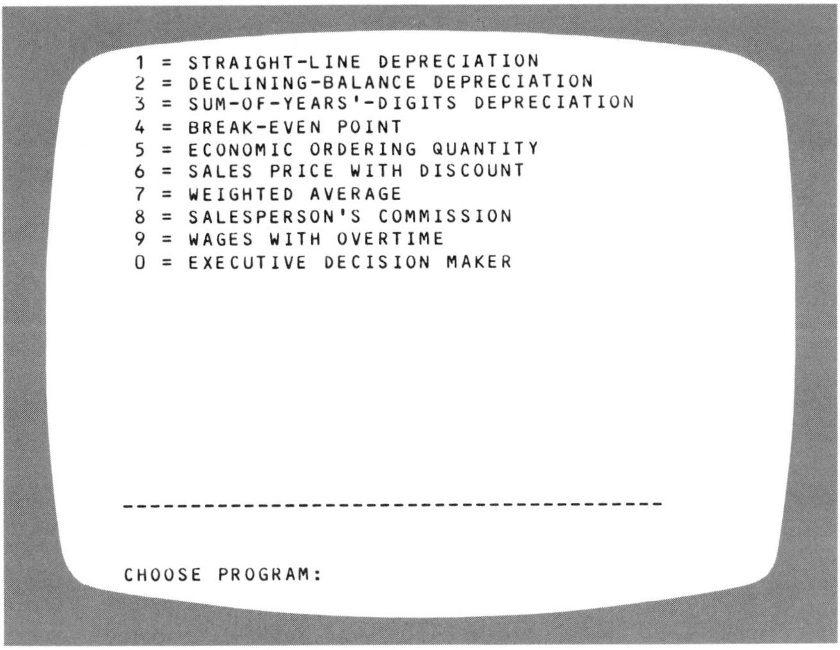

Figure 3.21: Screen Display: Business Programs Menu

```
100 REM -----------------------------
110 N$=      "BUSINESS PROGRAMS"
120 REM -----------------------------
130 GOSUB 6200: REM INITIALIZE
140 REM SET UP MENU ARRAY
150 X$(1)="STRAIGHT-LINE DEPRECIATION"
160 X$(2)="DECLINING-BALANCE DEPRECIATION"
170 X$(3)="SUM-OF-YEARS'-DIGITS DEPRECIATION"
180 X$(4)="BREAK-EVEN POINT"
190 X$(5)="ECONOMIC ORDERING QUANTITY"
200 X$(6)="SALES PRICE WITH DISCOUNT"
210 X$(7)="WEIGHTED AVERAGE"
220 X$(8)="SALESPERSON'S COMMISSION"
230 X$(9)="WAGES WITH OVERTIME"
240 X$(10)="EXECUTIVE DECISION MAKER"
250 N=10:GOSUB 7000: REM DISPLAY MENU
260 ON X GOSUB 280,500,740,1000,1160,1320,1540,1760,1930,2130
270 GOTO 100
```

Figure 3.22: Program Listing: Business Programs Menu

4

REAL ESTATE PROGRAMS

In this chapter we present eight useful real estate programs. These programs allow you to set up mortgage payment schedules and perform many other practical computations.

Two programs in this chapter are especially interesting. You can use the Affordable House Price program to find the sales price of a home that a bank will finance. This program is helpful both in finding a price range you can afford, and, should you decide to purchase, in negotiating a price. Another program you will find particularly enlightening is the Accelerated Payments program. A small increase in your monthly payment can drastically reduce the total interest you pay on a home. Take a look at Figure 4.8, and you'll see what we mean!

As in the other chapters, we provide a menu selection program that you can use to create a set of real estate programs.

REAL ESTATE SUBROUTINES

The programs in this chapter make use of three common subroutines. As usual, you should first load your subroutine library. Then enter and save these subroutines. When you are ready to enter a program, load the common subroutines. Then type in the program and save the subroutines and program together as a new file. You should enter all the programs in the chapter on the same file with these subroutines. The common subroutines are shown in Figure 4.1. These routines are used to get input for a payment calculation, calculate a payment, and compute the remaining balance of a loan.

```
250 REM -------------------------------
260 REM ROUTINE TO CALCULATE PAYMENT
270 REM -------------------------------
280 REM     CALLING PARAMETERS:
290 REM     IN=ANNUAL INTEREST RATE
300 REM     YR=NO. OF YEARS
310 REM     AM=AMOUNT OF LOAN
320 REM
330 N1=12*YR:I1=IN/100/12:V=1/(1+I1)
340 P=AM*I1/(1-V^N1)
350 RETURN
360 REM -------------------------------
370 REM GET INPUT FOR PAYMENT CALC
380 REM -------------------------------
390 Q1$="SPECIFY PARAMETERS":Q2$=""
400 Q3$="AMOUNT BORROWED ($)":GOSUB 6600
410 Q3$="ANNUAL INT RATE (%)":GOSUB 6600
420 Q3$="TERM OF LOAN (YRS)":GOSUB 6600
430 AM=P(1)
440 IN=P(2)
450 YR=P(3)
460 RETURN
470 REM -------------------------------
480 REM CALCULATE REMAINING BALANCE
490 REM -------------------------------
500 REM     CALLING PARAMETERS:
510 REM     P=PAYMENT
520 REM     IN=ANNUAL INTEREST RATE
530 REM     N=PAYMENT NUMBER
540 REM     AM=AMOUNT OF LOAN
550 FOR I=1 TO N
560 AM=AM-P+IN/12/100*AM
570 NEXT I
580 RETURN
```

Figure 4.1: Program Listing: Real Estate Subroutines

MONTHLY PAYMENT CALCULATION

Description

This program calculates the monthly payment necessary to fully amortize a loan. You must provide the amount of the loan, the annual interest rate, and the term of the loan in years.

Example

Don and Donna can purchase a house for $100,000. They plan to make a $25,000 down payment and finance the balance at 12% for 30 years. Find their monthly payment. Figures 4.2 and 4.3 show the screen display and the program listing for the Monthly Payment program.

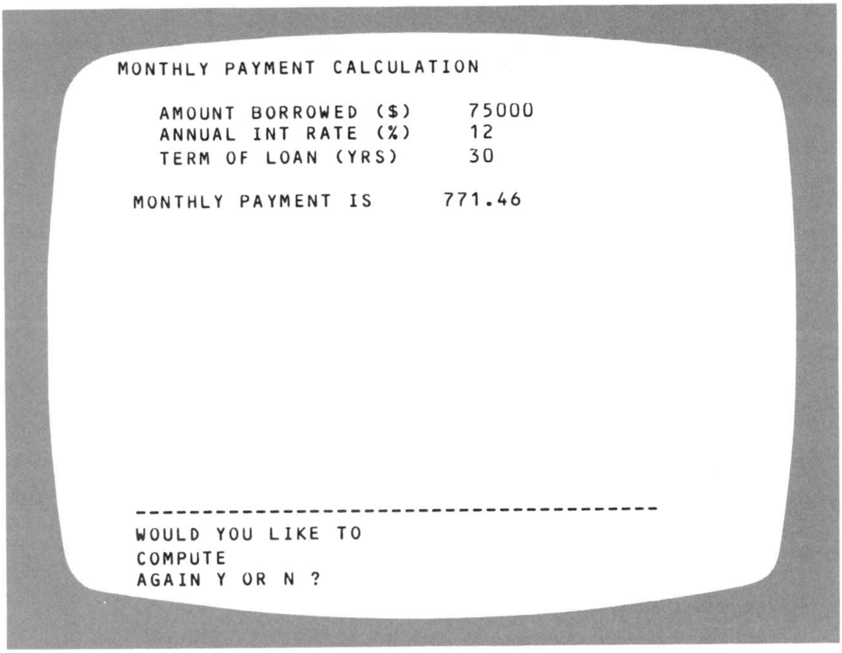

Figure 4.2: Screen Display: Monthly Payment Calculation

```
590 REM --------------------------------
600 N$= "MONTHLY PAYMENT CALCULATION"
610 REM --------------------------------
620 GOSUB 6200: K=1: REM INITIALIZE
630 GOSUB 360: REM GET PARAMETERS
640 GOSUB 250: REM CALCULATE PMT
650 PRINT
660 P=INT(P*100+.5)/100
670 PRINT"MONTHLY PAYMENT IS";TAB(22);P
680 Q2$="COMPUTE":GOSUB 3400: REM ASK FOR ANOTHER
690 IF YN$="N" THEN END
700 GOTO 590
```

Figure 4.3: Program Listing: Monthly Payment Calculation

MORTGAGE SCHEDULE

Description

This program displays a mortgage schedule on the screen for any year you choose. You enter the amount of the loan, the annual interest rate, the term of the loan, and the year for which you wish the mortgage schedule to be displayed. Thus, you can rapidly review the principal and interest you pay in any year. The interest you pay is deductible from your income tax.

Example

The mortgage on Sam and Samantha's home is $60,000. The annual interest rate is 11.5%, and the term of the loan is 25 years. Sam and Samantha would like to review the principal and interest they will be paying during the sixth year of the loan. Figure 4.4 shows the screen display for this example. The program listing is displayed in Figure 4.5.

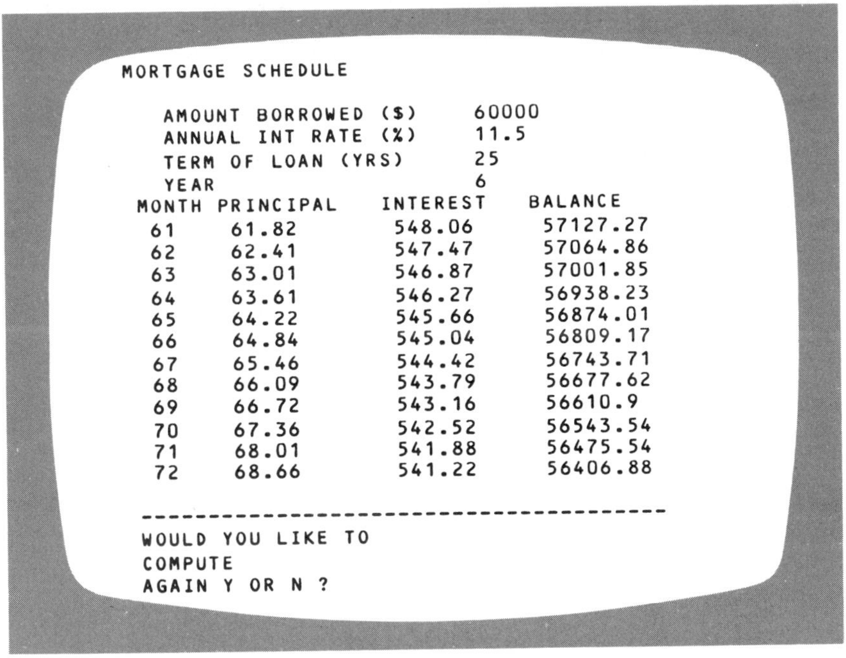

Figure 4.4: Screen Display: Mortgage Schedule

```
710 REM ------------------------------
720 N$=       "MORTGAGE SCHEDULE"
730 REM ------------------------------
740 GOSUB 6200: K=1: REM INITIALIZE
750 GOSUB 360: REM GET LOAN PARAMETERS
760 Q3$="YEAR":GOSUB 6600: N=P(4)
770 GOSUB 250: REM CALCULATE PAYMENT
780 N=12*N-12: REM COMPUTE FIRST MONTH
790 GOSUB 470: REM GET BEGINNING BALANCE
800 PRINT"MONTH PRINCIPAL   INTEREST   BALANCE"
810 FOR J=1 TO 12
820 I1=IN/12/100*AM: P1=P-I1: AM=AM-P1
830 N=N+1: I2=INT(I1*100+.5)/100
840 P2=INT(P1*100+.5)/100: A2=INT(AM*100+.5)/100
850 PRINT N;TAB(6);P2;TAB(18);I2;TAB(29);A2
860 NEXT J
870 Q2$="COMPUTE":GOSUB 3400: REM ASK FOR ANOTHER
880 IF YN$="N" THEN END
890 GOTO 710
```

Figure 4.5: Program Listing: Mortgage Schedule

REMAINING BALANCE OF A LOAN

Description

This program finds the remaining balance on a loan. You can run this program to calculate the amount due should you choose to pay off the loan. The program assumes that all prior payments have been the exact monthly payment. To use the program you specify the amount of the mortgage, the interest rate and length of the loan, and the payment number for which you want to determine the remaining balance. Don't be concerned if this program takes a while to display its answer.

Example

John's mortgage is $90,000. His loan is for 30 years at an annual interest rate of 9%. He would like to compute the loan balance at the end of five years (the sixtieth payment). Figures 4.6 and 4.7 show the screen display and the program listing for the Remaining Balance program.

```
REMAINING BALANCE

   AMOUNT BORROWED ($)     90000
   ANNUAL INT RATE (%)     9
   TERM OF LOAN (YRS)      30
   PAYMENT NUMBER          60

 MONTHLY PAYMENT         724.16
 BAL AFTER 60 PMTS       86292.12




 --------------------------------------
 WOULD YOU LIKE TO
 COMPUTE
 AGAIN Y OR N ?
```

Figure 4.6: Screen Display: Remaining Balance of a Loan

```
900 REM ------------------------------
910 N$=      "REMAINING BALANCE"
920 REM ------------------------------
930 GOSUB 6200: K=1
940 GOSUB 360: REM GET LOAN PARAMETERS
950 Q3$="PAYMENT NUMBER": GOSUB 6600: N=P(4)
960 GOSUB 250: REM CALCULATE PAYMENT
970 GOSUB 470: REM COMPUTE BALANCE
980 P=INT(P*100+.5)/100
990 AM=INT(AM*100+.5)/100: REM ROUND OFF
1000 PRINT
1010 PRINT"MONTHLY PAYMENT";TAB(22);P
1020 PRINT"BAL AFTER";N;"PMTS";TAB(22);AM
1030 Q2$="COMPUTE":GOSUB 3400: REM ASK FOR ANOTHER
1040 IF YN$="N" THEN END
1050 GOTO 900
```

Figure 4.7: Program Listing: Remaining Balance of a Loan

EFFECT OF ACCELERATED PAYMENTS

Description

You will find this program extremely useful—it allows you to find the effect of increasing the monthly payments on your mortgage. An increase in the monthly payments will reduce both the number of years of payments and the total interest you pay. To use this program, enter the amount of the loan, the annual interest rate, the length of the loan, the year in which you increase the payments, and the extra amount you will pay each month. This program computes as many times as necessary to reduce the loan balance to zero, so you may find that it takes a while for the answer to appear.

Example

Cindy has decided to increase the monthly payments on her home loan by $100 each month. She begins the increased payments in the seventh year of the loan and would like to know how much she will save on the interest. Her loan is for $60,000 at 9.75%; the term of her loan is 30 years. You can see in Figure 4.8 that Cindy will save $41,000 with this increase in her monthly payment, and she will reduce the term of the loan by about 9½ years. Figure 4.9 shows the program listing for the Accelerated Payments program.

```
1060 REM ----------------------------
1070 N$=    "ACCELERATED PAYMENTS"
1080 REM ----------------------------
1090 GOSUB 6200: K=1: REM INITIALIZE
1100 GOSUB 360: REM GET LOAN PARAMETERS
1110 Q3$="YEAR OF INCREASE":GOSUB 6600: N=P(4)
1120 GOSUB 250: REM CALCULATE PAYMENT
1130 N=12*N-12: REM COMPUTE FIRST MONTH
1140 Q3$="EXTRA AMOUNT PAID ($)": GOSUB 6600: EX=P(5)
1150 REM COMPUTE PRIN INT AND BAL TO DATE
1160 T=0:BAL=0:TP=0
1170 FOR J=1 TO N
1180 I1=IN/12/100*AM:P1=P-I1:AM=AM-P1
1190 T=T+I1: TP=TP+P1
1200 NEXT J
```

Figure 4.9: Program Listing: Effect of Accelerated Payments (continues)

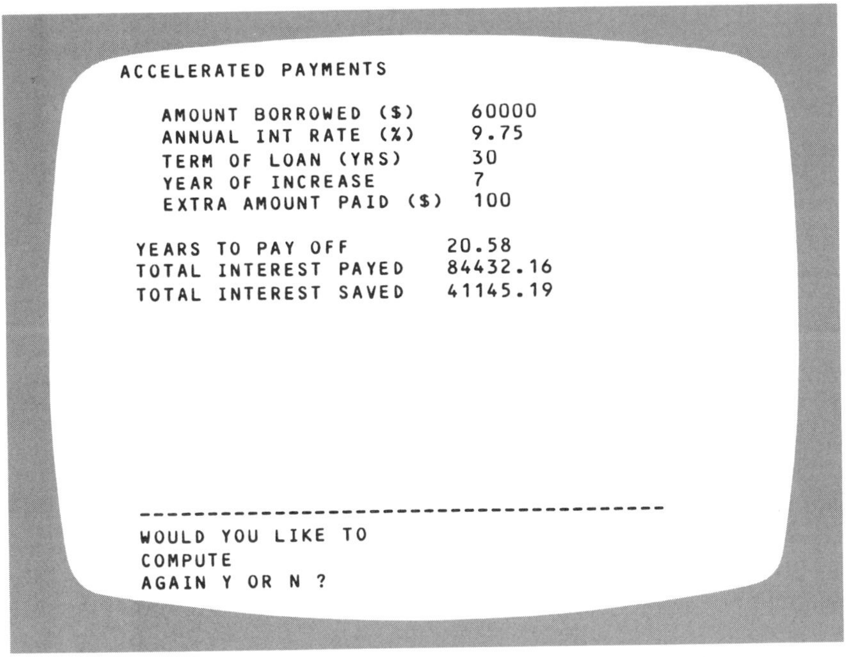

Figure 4.8: Screen Display: Effect of Accelerated Payments

```
1210 REM COMPUTE INTEREST WITH NO INCREASE
1220 T2=0:A2=P(1)
1230 FOR J=1 TO 12*YR
1240 I2=IN/12/100*A2:P2=P-I2:A2=A2-P2
1250 T2=T2+I2
1260 NEXT J
1270 REM COMPUTE WITH XTRA PAYMENT
1280 J=0
1290 I1=IN/12/100*AM: T=T+I1
1300 P1=P+EX-I1: TP=TP+P1
1310 AM=AM-P1
1320 J=J+1
1330 IF AM>0 THEN 1290
1340 YR=INT((P(4)+J/12-1)*100+.5)/100
1350 T=INT(T*100+.5)/100
1360 T2=INT((T2-T)*100+.5)/100
1370 PRINT
1380 PRINT"YEARS TO PAY OFF";TAB(22);YR
1390 PRINT"TOTAL INTEREST PAYED";TAB(22);T
1400 PRINT"TOTAL INTEREST SAVED";TAB(22);T2
1410 Q2$="COMPUTE":GOSUB 3400
1420 IF YN$="N" THEN END
1430 GOTO 1060
```

Figure 4.9: Program Listing: Effect of Accelerated Payments

BALLOON PAYMENT CALCULATION

Description

Many recent mortgages have been set up with a balloon payment due at the end of a specified period. This program allows you to calculate the required balloon payment. You must enter the amount of the loan, the annual interest rate, the term of the loan, and the year in which the balloon payment is due.

Example

Max has a mortgage for $125,000. The annual interest rate is 11%. The payments are amortized over 30 years; Max must pay off the entire loan at the end of 10 years. What will be the amount of Max's balloon payment? Figures 4.10 and 4.11 show the screen display and the program listing for the Balloon Payment program.

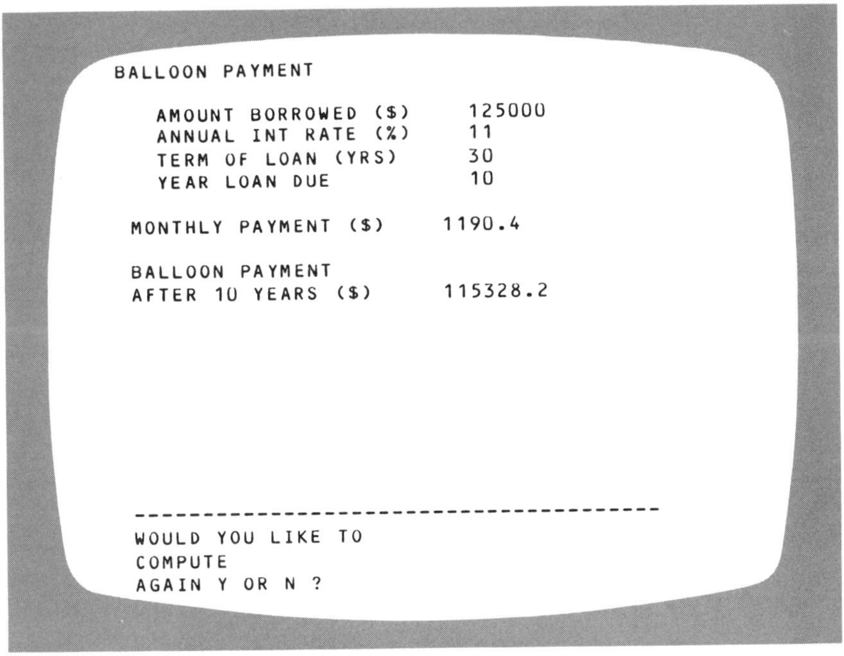

Figure 4.10: Screen Display: Balloon Payment Calculation

```
1440 REM ------------------------------
1450 N$=       "BALLOON PAYMENT"
1460 REM ------------------------------
1470 GOSUB 6200: K=1: REM INITIALIZE
1480 GOSUB 360: REM GET LOAN PARAMETERS
1490 Q3$="YEAR LOAN DUE": GOSUB 6600: N=12*P(4)
1500 GOSUB 250: REM CALCULATE PAYMENT
1510 GOSUB 470: REM COMPUTE BALANCE
1520 P=INT(P*100+.5)/100
1530 YR=INT(N/12*100+.5)/100
1540 AM=INT(AM*100+.5)/100
1550 PRINT:PRINT"MONTHLY PAYMENT ($)";TAB(22);P
1560 PRINT:PRINT"BALLOON PAYMENT"
1570 PRINT"AFTER";YR;"YEARS ($)";TAB(22);AM
1580 Q2$="COMPUTE":GOSUB 3400:REM ASK FOR ANOTHER
1590 IF YN$="N" THEN END
1600 GOTO 1440
```

Figure 4.11: Program Listing: Balloon Payment Calculation

AFFORDABLE HOUSE PRICE

Description

You can use this program to find the price of a home for which a bank will give you a loan. This program can be invaluable when you are negotiating to buy a new home. To use the program, enter the annual interest rate and term of available loans, your annual income, the estimated annual taxes and insurance, the percent of your gross income that the bank will allow for your total monthly payments, and the percent down payment you will make.

Example

Bill and Betty would like to purchase a new home. The available interest rate for home loans is 13.5% for 30-year loans. The couple's annual income is $50,000 per year, and they plan to put 20% down on their new house. Bill and Betty estimate that their yearly taxes and insurance will be $2,400. Their banker has told them that the monthly payment on their house must not exceed 35% of their monthly income. Figures 4.12 and 4.13 are the screen display and the program listing for the Affordable House Price program.

```
AFFORDABLE HOUSE PRICE

  ANNUAL INT RATE (%)      13.5
  TERM OF LOAN (YRS)       30
  BUYER'S ANNUAL INC       50000
  EST ANNUAL TAX & INS     2400
  % OF INC FOR PAYMENTS    35
  % DOWN PAYMENT           20

 AMOUNT FINANCED ($)     109858.56
 AFFORDABLE HOUSE ($)    137323.2




 ----------------------------------------
 WOULD YOU LIKE TO
 COMPUTE
 AGAIN Y OR N ?
```

Figure 4.12: Screen Display: Affordable House Price

```
1610 REM ----------------------------
1620 N$=    "AFFORDABLE HOUSE PRICE"
1630 REM ----------------------------
1640 GOSUB 6200: K=1: REM INITIALIZE
1650 Q1$="SPECIFY PARAMETERS":Q2$=""
1660 Q3$="ANNUAL INT RATE (%)":GOSUB 6600
1670 Q3$="TERM OF LOAN (YRS)":GOSUB 6600
1680 Q3$="BUYER'S ANNUAL INC":GOSUB 6600
1690 Q3$="EST ANNUAL TAX & INS":GOSUB 6600
1700 Q3$="% OF INC FOR PAYMENTS":GOSUB 6600
1710 Q3$="% DOWN PAYMENT":GOSUB 6600
1720 PRINT
1730 REM COMPUTE ALLOWABLE PAYMENT
1740 P=P(5)/100*P(3)/12-P(4)/12
1750 REM COMPUTE AMOUNT FINANCED
1760 IN=P(1)/100/12:N1=12*P(2):V=1/(1+IN)
1770 AM=INT(P*(1-V^N1)/IN*100+.5)/100
1780 AH=INT(AM/(1-P(6)/100)*100+.5)/100
1790 PRINT"AMOUNT FINANCED ($)";TAB(22);AM
1800 PRINT"AFFORDABLE HOUSE ($)";TAB(22);AH
1810 Q2$="COMPUTE":GOSUB 3400:REM ASK FOR ANOTHER
1820 IF YN$="N" THEN END
1830 GOTO 1610
```

Figure 4.13: Program Listing: Affordable House Price

MORTGAGE WITH SECOND MORTGAGE

Description

We shall now examine a program you can use to find the total payments on a house that will have both a first and second mortgage. To use this program you enter the purchase price of the home, the cash available for a down payment, and the amount of the first mortgage you will obtain. You also specify the interest rate of the first and second mortgages and the length of the first. We assume that the second mortgage is paid monthly on an interest-only basis.

Example

Joanne has saved $20,000 for a down payment on a new house. The house will cost $140,000 and she plans to take out a first mortgage for $90,000. The first mortgage will be for 30 years at 12% annual interest. She will also have a 16% interest-only second mortgage. What will be her total payments? The resulting screen display for this example is shown in Figure 4.14; the program listing appears in Figure 4.15.

```
1840 REM -----------------------------
1850 N$=    "MORTGAGE WITH SECOND"
1860 REM -----------------------------
1870 GOSUB 6200: K=1
1880 Q1$="SPECIFY PARAMETERS":Q2$=""
```

Figure 4.15: Program Listing: Mortgage with Second Mortgage (continues)

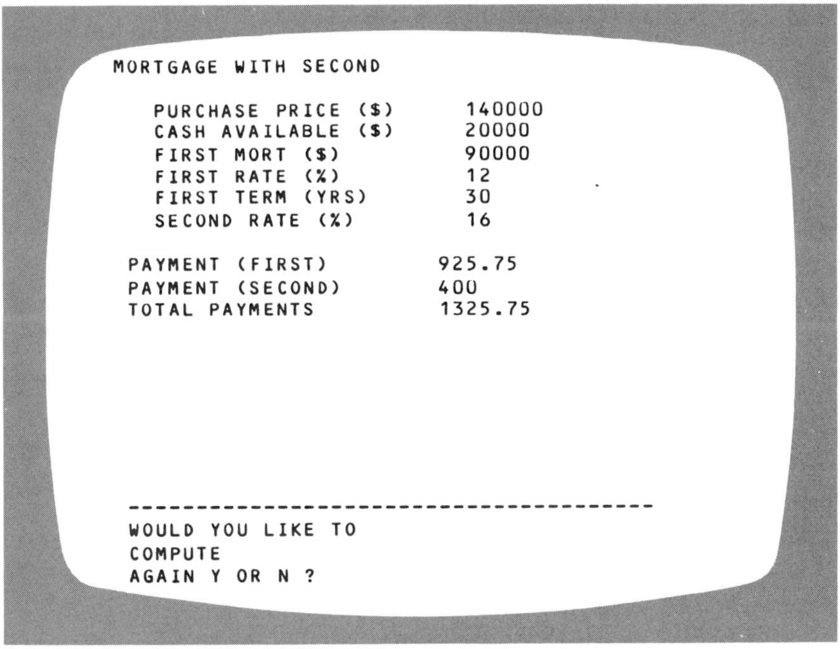

Figure 4.14: Screen Display: Mortgage with Second Mortgage

```
1890 Q3$="PURCHASE PRICE ($)":GOSUB 6600
1900 Q3$="CASH AVAILABLE ($)":GOSUB 6600
1910 Q3$="FIRST MORT ($)":GOSUB 6600
1920 Q3$="FIRST RATE (%)":GOSUB 6600
1930 Q3$="FIRST TERM (YRS)":GOSUB 6600
1940 Q3$="SECOND RATE (%)":GOSUB 6600
1950 PRINT
1960 AM=P(3):IN=P(4):YR=P(5)
1970 REM COMPUTE FIRST PAYMENT
1980 GOSUB 250:P=INT(P*100+.5)/100
1990 PRINT"PAYMENT (FIRST)";TAB(22);P
2000 REM COMPUTE SECOND PAYMENT
2010 IF P(2)<P(1)-P(3) THEN 2040
2020 PRINT"SECOND MORTGAGE NOT REQUIRED"
2030 GOTO 2070
2040 P2=INT((P(1)-P(2)-P(3))*P(6)/12+.5)/100
2050 PRINT"PAYMENT (SECOND)";TAB(22);P2
2060 PRINT"TOTAL PAYMENTS";TAB(22);P+P2
2070 Q2$="COMPUTE":GOSUB 3400
2080 IF YN$="N" THEN END
2090 GOTO 1840
```

Figure 4.15: Program Listing: Mortgage with Second Mortgage

RENTAL PROPERTY ANALYSIS

Description

Let's now consider a program that is very useful for analyzing real estate investments. You can use the Rental Property Analysis program to find the monthly payment and cash flow on a rental property. (We don't consider the after-tax effects of depreciation.) You must enter the amount of the loan on your rental property, the annual interest rate and length of the loan, and the annual insurance, taxes, and maintenance. You must also enter the monthly rental income.

Example

Herb is planning to purchase a house, which he will rent for $475 per month. The first mortgage will be $80,000, amortized over 30 years at 12% interest. Herb estimates that the annual insurance will be $500, the property taxes $1,600, and the maintenance $400. What will be his monthly payment and cash flow? Figures 4.16 and 4.17 are the screen display and program listing for this example.

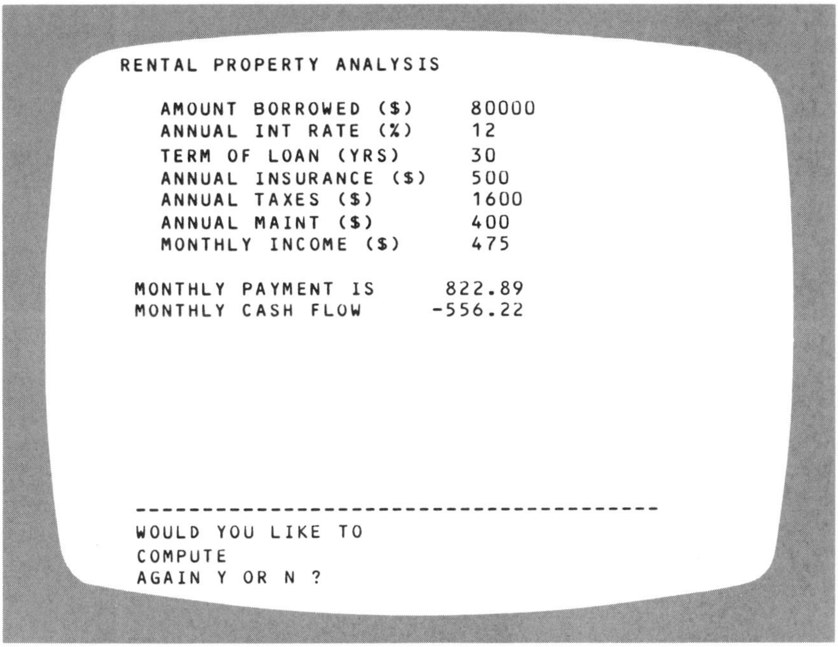

Figure 4.16: Screen Display: Rental Property Analysis

```
2100 REM -----------------------------
2110 N$=  "RENTAL PROPERTY ANALYSIS"
2120 REM -----------------------------
2130 GOSUB 6200: K=1
2140 REM GET PARAMETERS
2160 GOSUB 360
2170 Q3$="ANNUAL INSURANCE ($)":GOSUB 6600
2180 Q3$="ANNUAL TAXES ($)":GOSUB 6600
2190 Q3$="ANNUAL MAINT ($)":GOSUB 6600
2200 Q3$="MONTHLY INCOME ($)":GOSUB 6600
2210 GOSUB 250: REM CALCULATE PMT
2220 PRINT
2230 P=INT(P*100+.5)/100
2240 PRINT"MONTHLY PAYMENT IS";TAB(22);P
2250 CF=INT((P(7)-P-(P(4)+P(5)+P(6))/12)*100+.5)/100
2260 PRINT"MONTHLY CASH FLOW";TAB(22);CF
2270 Q2$="COMPUTE":GOSUB 3400
2280 IF YN$="N" THEN END
2290 GOTO 2100
```

Figure 4.17: Program Listing: Rental Property Analysis

REAL ESTATE PROGRAMS MENU

We can again combine the programs in this chapter to provide a menu-driven real estate analysis package. Remember to replace the END command in each program with a RETURN command. Instructions for combining and saving the menu program are in Chapter 2. The menu display and its program listing are shown in Figures 4.18 and 4.19.

[redacted]

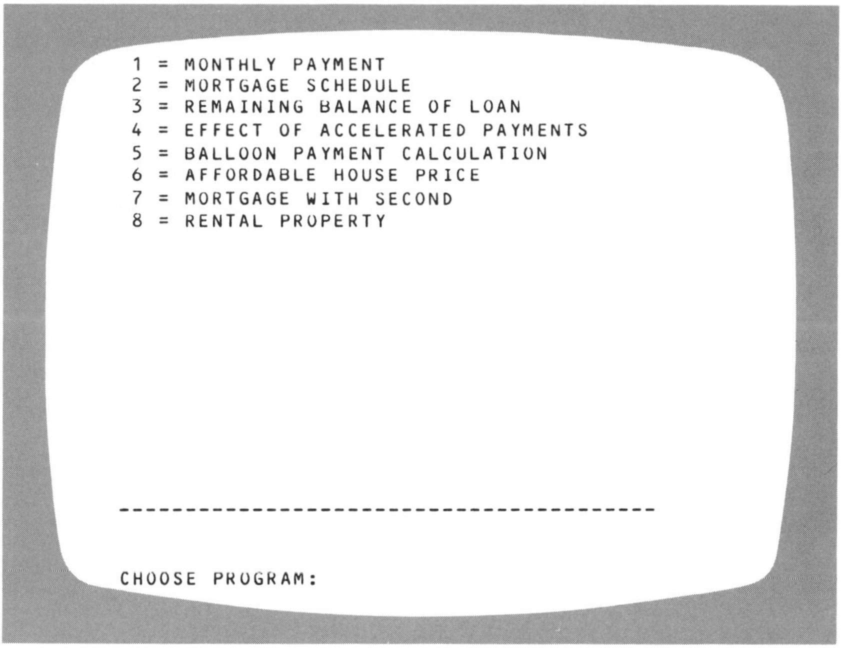

Figure 4.18: Screen Display: Real Estate Programs Menu

```
100 REM ------------------------------
110 N$=     "REAL ESTATE PROGRAMS"
120 REM ------------------------------
130 GOSUB 6200: REM INITIALIZE
140 X$(1)="MONTHLY PAYMENT"
150 X$(2)="MORTGAGE SCHEDULE"
160 X$(3)="REMAINING BALANCE OF LOAN"
170 X$(4)="EFFECT OF ACCELERATED PAYMENTS"
180 X$(5)="BALLOON PAYMENT CALCULATION"
190 X$(6)="AFFORDABLE HOUSE PRICE"
200 X$(7)="MORTGAGE WITH SECOND"
210 X$(8)="RENTAL PROPERTY"
220 N=8:GOSUB 7000: REM DISPLAY MENU
230 ON X GOSUB 590,710,900,1060,1440,1610,1840,2100
240 GOTO 100
```

Figure 4.19: Program Listing: Real Estate Programs Menu

5

DATA ANALYSIS PROGRAMS

This chapter describes a set of data analysis programs that you can use to reduce and plot various kinds of data. We present programs that input data, plot it on the screen, compute moving averages, and perform linear regression analyses. The Plot Data program will also plot data that are reduced by the programs in this chapter.

Investors, among others, will find the data analysis programs very useful. You can input daily stock prices and then try the various smoothing programs. These programs smooth out daily price variations and give an indication of longer term trends. The data analysis programs can also be used in many other situations, including analyzing scientific data, plotting and smoothing weight variations, and tracking weather data.

The programs in this and the following two chapters require that you first enter the menu program and additional common subroutines. You should save these programs in one file after they are entered; you then add the other programs as described in Chapter 1. Because the programs in these chapters *begin* with the menu program, you don't have to change any lines within the programs to activate the menu.

DATA ANALYSIS PROGRAMS MENU

The data analysis programs all work together through common arrays and a common menu program. Notice that the menu lists an input program, a plot program, and several analysis programs. You use the programs together by first entering data with the input program. You can then plot the data or analyze it. Input data are stored in the array D. Data you reduce with the analysis programs are stored in the array R.

After you run each program you return to the menu. You can then analyze the data again with a different program; you can plot input data, reduced data, or both; or you can enter new data.

Figure 5.1 shows the screen display of the Data Analysis Menu. Figure 5.2 shows the menu program listing.

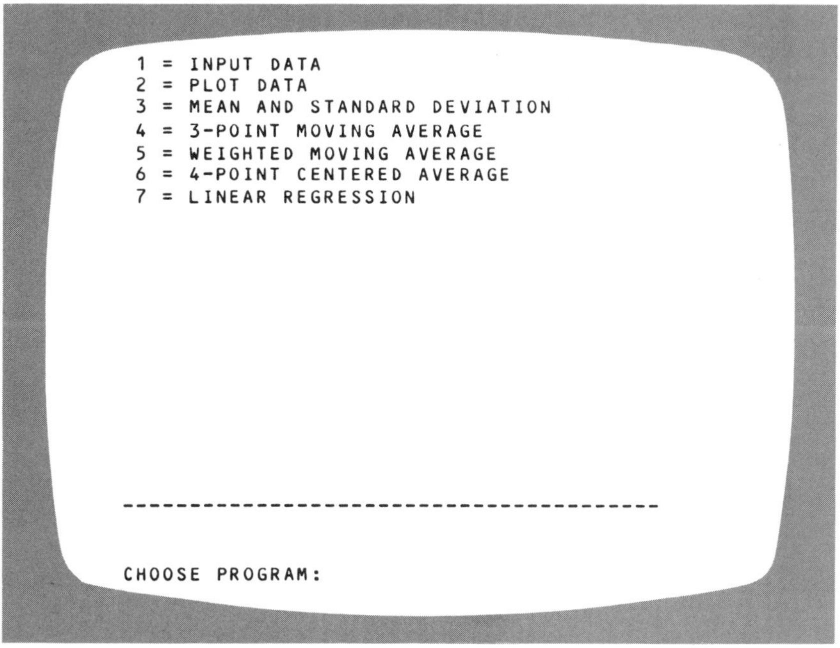

Figure 5.1: Screen Display: Data Analysis Menu

```
100 REM ------------------------------
110 N$=     "DATA ANALYSIS PROGRAMS"
120 REM ------------------------------
130 DIM R(40),D(40)
135 D(4)=5
140 GOSUB 6200: REM INITIALIZE
150 REM SET UP MENU
160 X$(1)="INPUT DATA"
170 X$(2)="PLOT DATA"
180 X$(3)="MEAN AND STANDARD DEVIATION"
190 X$(4)="3-POINT MOVING AVERAGE"
200 X$(5)="WEIGHTED MOVING AVERAGE"
210 X$(6)="4-POINT CENTERED AVERAGE"
220 X$(7)="LINEAR REGRESSION"
230 N=7:GOSUB 7000: REM DISPLAY MENU
240 ON X GOSUB 630,810,1050,1270,1470,1670,1870
250 GOTO 140
```

Figure 5.2: Program Listing: Data Analysis Menu

DATA ANALYSIS SUBROUTINES

The Plot Data program uses two subroutines to plot data on the screen. One routine draws the axes; the other scales and plots the data. You must enter these programs prior to using the plot program. Figure 5.3 is the program listing for the axis subroutine.

Figure 5.4 shows the program listing for the routine that scales and plots the data. This program plots either input data, reduced data, or both input and reduced data, depending on the user-controlled variable CH$.

```
270 REM ------------------------------
280 REM           DRAW AXES
290 REM ------------------------------
300 PRINT CHR$(147);: REM CLEAR SCREEN
310 X=6:FOR Y=1 TO 21: REM Y AXIS
320 GOSUB 4200: PRINT" I"
330 NEXT Y: FOR Y=1 TO 16 STEP 5
340 X=6:GOSUB 4200: PRINT"-";: X=1: GOSUB 4200
350 PRINT INT(MX-(MX-MN)/4*(Y-1)/5);
360 NEXT Y: X=8:Y=21: GOSUB 4200
370 FOR X=1 TO 32: REM X AXIS
380 PRINT"-";
390 NEXT X
400 FOR I=8 TO 38 STEP 5: REM X AXIS TICKS
410 Y=21:X=I:GOSUB 4200: PRINT"I";
420 Y=22:X=I-1: GOSUB 4200: PRINT I-7;
430 NEXT I
440 RETURN
```

Figure 5.3: Program Listing: Axis Subroutine

```
470 REM ------------------------------
480 REM       SCALE DATA AND PLOT IT
490 REM ------------------------------
500 FOR I=1 TO ND
510 P1=21-INT(20*(D(I)-MN)/(MX-MN))
520 P2=21-INT(20*(R(I)-MN)/(MX-MN))
530 IF CH$<>"I" AND CH$<>"B" THEN 570
540 IF P1>21 OR P1<1 THEN 620
550 Y=P1:X=I+7:GOSUB 4200: PRINT"*";
570 IF CH$<>"R" AND CH$<>"B" THEN 600
580 IF P2>21 OR P2<1 THEN 620
590 X=I+7: Y=P2:GOSUB 4200: PRINT"+";
600 NEXT I
610 RETURN
620 ERF=1:RETURN
```

Figure 5.4: Program Listing: Scale and Plot Subroutine

INPUT DATA

Description

You use this program to enter data that the other programs analyze and plot. You can enter up to 32 data points with the Input Data program. The data are stored in the array D(I). The program prompts you to enter data in the order of their occurrence. If you enter fewer than 32 data points, you type a D to signify that you are done entering data. The input screen is set up to display the last ten points that you enter, so you can check yourself as you go along. Remember, all data that you smooth and plot must first be entered with the Input Data program.

Example

Mary Ann would like to input the data she obtained in a laboratory experiment. The data are as follows:

Point	1	2	3	4	5	6	7	8	9	10
Data	1	3	5	4	4	5	7	8	9	11
Point	11	12	13	14	15	16	17	18	19	20
Data	12	15	13	14	15	16	15	13	12	12
Point	21	22	23	24	25	26	27	28	29	30
Data	11	10	7	9	8	7	5	5	4	3
Point	31	32								
Data	3	0								

Figure 5.5 shows the screen display; Figure 5.6 contains the program listing for the Input Data program.

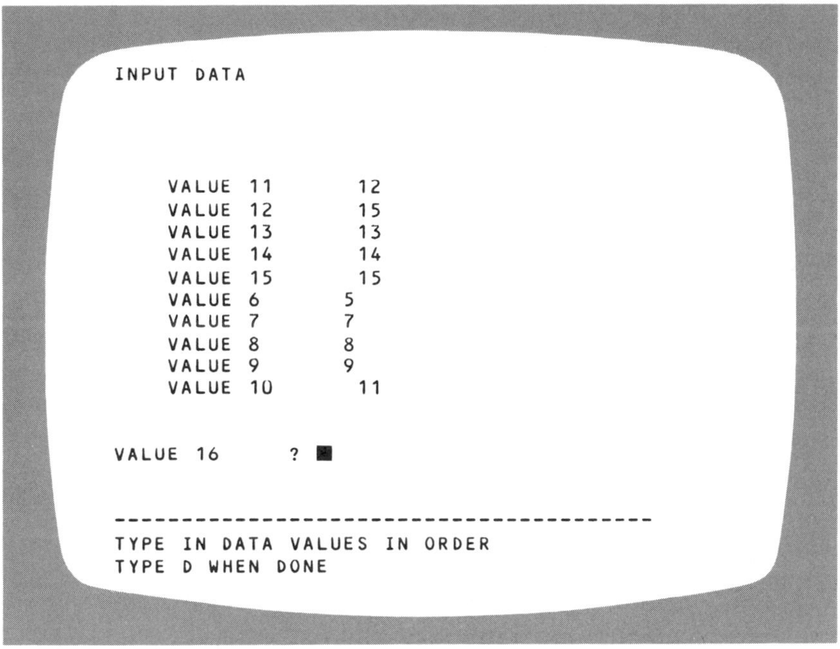

Figure 5.5: Screen Display: Input Data

```
630 REM ------------------------------
640 N$=          "INPUT DATA"
650 REM ------------------------------
660 GOSUB 6200: REM INITIALIZE
670 Q1$="TYPE IN DATA VALUES IN ORDER"
680 Q2$="TYPE D WHEN DONE"
690 Q3$="": GOSUB 5000: REM DIALOG
700 ND=0: REM NUMBER OF DATA POINTS
710 ND=ND+1: IF ND>32 THEN 800
720 X=1: Y=18: GOSUB 4200: PRINT S$: GOSUB 4200
730 PRINT"VALUE";ND;"    ";: INPUT E$
740 IF E$="D" THEN 790
745 PRINT:PRINT
750 X=5:Y=ND-INT((ND-1)/10)*10+5
760 GOSUB 4200: PRINT S$: GOSUB 4200
770 PRINT"VALUE";ND;"     ";E$
780 D(ND)=VAL(E$):GOTO 710
790 ND=ND-1
800 RETURN
```

Figure 5.6: Program Listing: Input Data

PLOT DATA

Description

The Plot Data program plots either input data or reduced data on the screen. (Reduced data result from using the data analysis programs that follow.) You must tell the program to plot input data, reduced data (data on which you have run one of the data analysis programs), or both by answering the program prompt with an I, R, or B respectively. The * symbol represents input data, and the + symbol represents reduced data. You must also specify the maximum and minimum Y-axis scale values. If your input data exceed your scale values, you will get the message DATA OUT OF RANGE. You must then respecify the scale values.

Example

Let's now plot the input data from the previous example. In this case we choose a maximum value of 20 and a minimum value of 0. We choose to plot input data (I), because we have not reduced it yet. Figure 5.7 shows the screen display for the data plot. Figure 5.8 displays the Plot Data program listing.

```
810 REM ------------------------------
820 N$=      "PLOT DATA ROUTINE"
830 REM ------------------------------
840 Q1$="":Q2$="INPUT OR REDUCED OR BOTH"
```

Figure 5.8: Program Listing: Plot Data (continues)

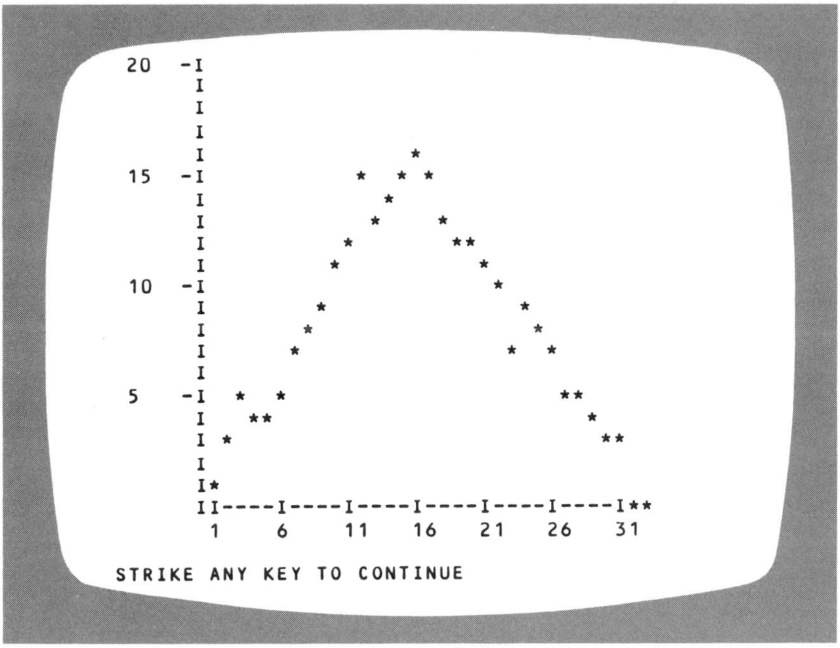

Figure 5.7: Screen Display: Plot Data

```
850 Q3$="DATA (I OR R OR B)"
860 GOSUB 5000
870 GOSUB 5400: REM GET CHAR
880 IF CH$<>"I" AND CH$<>"R" AND CH$<>"B" THEN 870
890 Q2$=""
900 Q3$="CHOOSE MAX SCALE: "
910 GOSUB 5000: INPUT MX
920 Q3$="CHOOSE MIN SCALE: "
930 GOSUB 5000: INPUT MN
940 GOSUB 270: REM DRAW AXES
950 ERF=0
960 GOSUB 470: REM PLOT DATA
970 IF ERF=0 THEN 1010
980 Q1$="DATA OUT OF RANGE"
990 Q2$="PLEASE RESPECIFY"
1000 GOTO 900
1010 X=1:Y=24: GOSUB 4200
1020 PRINT"STRIKE ANY KEY TO CONTINUE";
1030 GET CH$: IF CH$="" THEN 1030
1040 RETURN
```

Figure 5.8: Program Listing: Plot Data

MEAN AND STANDARD DEVIATION

Description

We shall now look at a program that computes the mean and standard deviation for data that have been input with the Input Data program. To use this program you simply select it from the Data Analysis Menu.

Example

Mary Ann would like to compute the mean and standard deviation for the laboratory data she has input. She runs the program and displays the results in Figure 5.9. The program listing for this example appears in Figure 5.10.

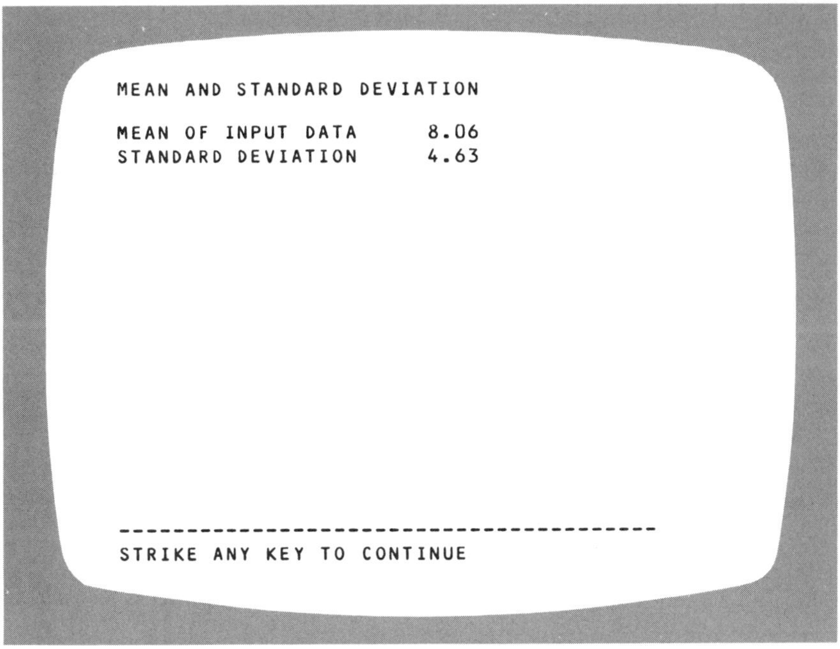

Figure 5.9: Screen Display: Mean and Standard Deviation

```
1050 REM ----------------------------
1060 N$= "MEAN AND STANDARD DEVIATION"
1070 REM ----------------------------
1080 GOSUB 6200
1090 REM COMPUTE THE MEAN
1100 ME=0
1110 FOR I=1 TO ND
1120 ME=ME+D(I)
1130 NEXT I
1140 ME=ME/ND
1150 REM COMPUTE THE STANDARD DEVIATION
1160 SD=0
1170 FOR I=1 TO ND
1180 SD=SD+(D(I)-ME)^2
1190 NEXT I
1200 SD=(SD/ND)^.5
1210 ME=INT(ME*100+.5)/100
1220 SD=INT(SD*100+.5)/100
1230 PRINT "MEAN OF INPUT DATA";TAB(22);ME
1240 PRINT"STANDARD DEVIATION";TAB(22);SD
1250 GOSUB 7400
1260 RETURN
```

Figure 5.10: Program Listing: Mean and Standard Deviation

THREE-POINT MOVING AVERAGE

Description

We shall now present three data smoothing programs. The first program computes a three-point moving average on data you store in the Input Data array. The smoothed data are stored in the array R(I). You can display the smoothed data in either numeric or graph form. The three-point moving average takes the average value of the three prior data points and uses the average as the smoothed result. After the program smooths the data, it will ask:

```
DO YOU WANT TO PRINT THE DATA
```

If you answer with a Y, the program displays the data in numeric form. When you return to the main menu, you can graph the smoothed data with the Plot Data program. If you answer with an N, the program returns immediately to the main menu, so that you can run the Plot Data program.

Example

Mary Ann would like to try various smoothing techniques on her laboratory data. She first runs the Three-Point Moving Average program and graphs the results together with the input data. You can see the smoothed data in Figure 5.11; wherever the input data and smoothed data are the same, only the smoothed data are shown. The program listing is shown in Figure 5.12.

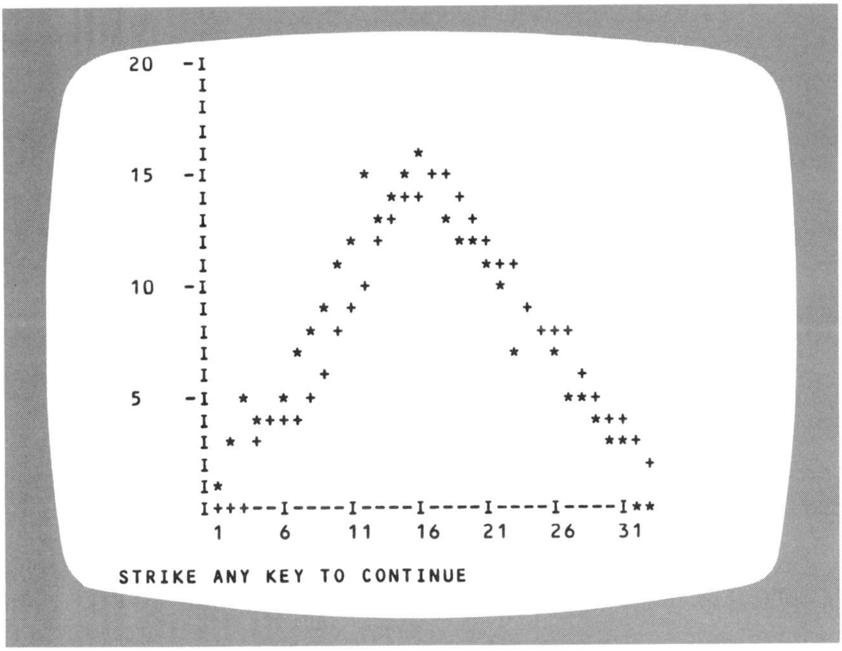

Figure 5.11: Screen Display: Three-Point Moving Average

```
1270 REM ------------------------------
1280 N$=    "3-POINT MOVING AVERAGE"
1290 REM ------------------------------
1300 GOSUB 6200: REM INITIALIZE
1310 REM SET UP RESULT IN R(I)
1320 R(1)=0: R(2)=0: R(3)=0
1330 FOR I=4 TO ND
1340 R(I)=(D(I-3)+D(I-2)+D(I-1))/3
1350 NEXT I
1360 Q1$="DO YOU WANT TO PRINT THE"
1370 Q2$="DATA (Y OR N)"
1380 Q3$="": GOSUB 5000
1390 GOSUB 7800: REM ASK YES OR NO
1400 IF YN$="N" THEN RETURN
1410 PRINT CHR$(147);: REM CLEAR SCREEN
1420 FOR I=4 TO ND
1425 R(I)=INT((R(I)+.005)*100)/100
1430 PRINT R(I),
1440 NEXT I
1450 GOSUB 7400: REM PAUSE
1460 RETURN

READY.
```

Figure 5.12: Program Listing: Three-Point Moving Average

WEIGHTED MOVING AVERAGE

Description

A second smoothing technique is the three-point weighted average. We smooth the data by weighting the most recent point by three, the second most recent point by two, and the third most recent point by one. Thus, the most recent point is given the highest weight. You use this program by calling it from the menu; the resulting data are stored in the array R(I). Again, the data can be displayed numerically or graphed by the Plot Data program. Note that only one set of reduced data can be stored at a time.

Example

Let's use the weighted average program with Mary Ann's laboratory data. In Figure 5.13 we plot both the input data and the reduced data resulting from the Weighted Moving Average program. The program listing is given in Figure 5.14.

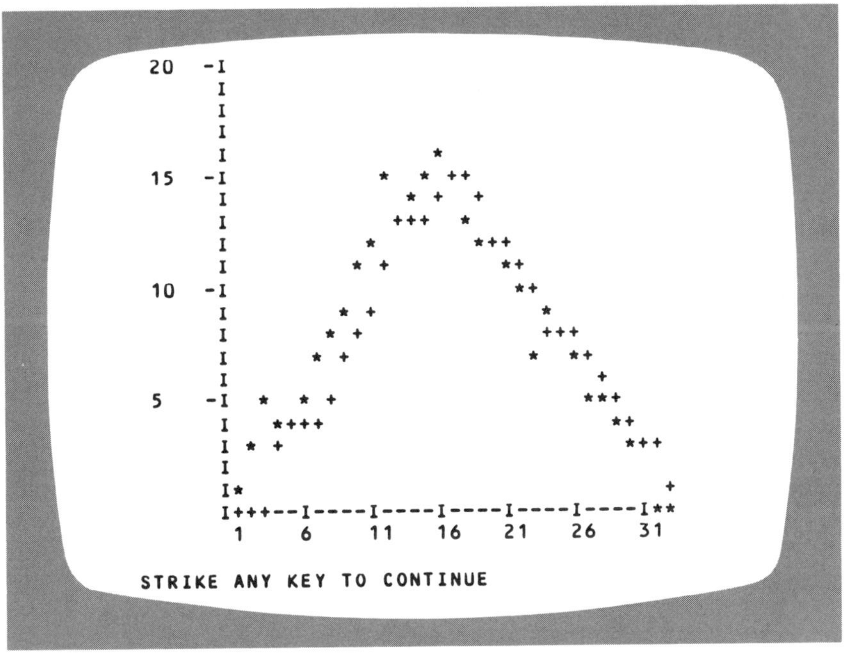

Figure 5.13: Screen Display: Weighted Moving Average

```
1470 REM ------------------------------
1480 N$="3-PT. WEIGHTED MOVING AVERAGE"
1490 REM ------------------------------
1500 GOSUB 6200: REM INITIALIZE
1510 REM SET UP RESULT IN R(I)
1520 R(1)=0:R(2)=0:R(3)=0
1530 FOR I=4 TO ND
1540 R(I)=(D(I-3)+2*D(I-2)+3*D(I-1))/6
1550 NEXT I
1560 Q1$="DO YOU WANT TO PRINT THE"
1570 Q2$="DATA (Y OR N)"
1580 Q3$="": GOSUB 5000
1590 GOSUB 7800
1600 IF YN$="N" THEN RETURN
1610 PRINT CHR$(147)
1620 FOR I=4 TO ND
1625 R(I)=INT((R(I)+.005)*100)/100
1630 PRINT R(I),
1640 NEXT I
1650 GOSUB 7400: REM PAUSE
1660 RETURN

READY.
```

Figure 5.14: Program Listing: Weighted Moving Average

FOUR-POINT CENTERED AVERAGE

Description

We now review a final smoothing technique, the four-point centered average. This technique weights the first and fifth most recent points by a factor of one and the second, third, and fourth most recent points by a factor of two. You use this program by selecting it from the menu. You can list the smoothed data or plot it with the Plot Data program.

Example

Let's apply the centered-average technique to Mary Ann's laboratory data. Figure 5.15 shows the smoothed data along with the input data. Figure 5.16 shows the program listing.

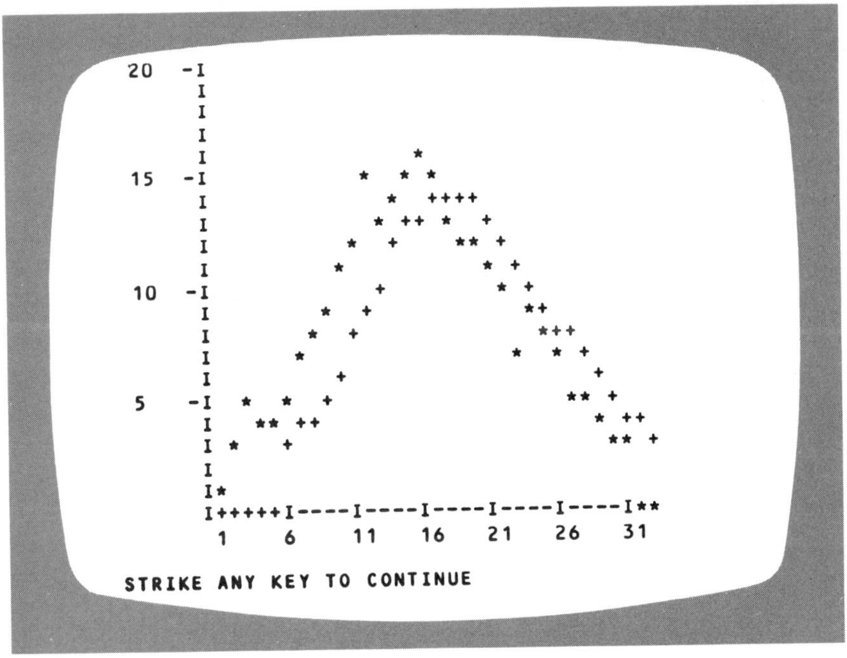

Figure 5.15: Screen Display: Four-Point Centered Average

```
1670 REM ------------------------------
1680 N$=   "4-PT. CENTERED AVERAGE"
1690 REM ------------------------------
1700 GOSUB 6200: REM INITIALIZE
1710 REM SET UP RESULT IN R(I)
1720 R(1)=0:R(2)=0:R(3)=0:R(4)=0:R(5)=0
1730 FOR I=6 TO ND
1740 R(I)=(D(I-5)+2*(D(I-4)+D(I-3)+D(I-2))+D(I-1))/8
1750 NEXT I
1760 Q1$="DO YOU WANT TO PRINT THE"
1770 Q2$="DATA (Y OR N)"
1780 Q3$="": GOSUB 5000
1790 GOSUB 7800: REM ASK YES OR NO
1800 IF YN$="N" THEN RETURN
1810 PRINT CHR$(147)
1820 FOR I=4 TO ND
1825 R(I)=INT((R(I)+.005)*100)/100
1830 PRINT R(I),
1840 NEXT I
1850 GOSUB 7400: REM PAUSE
1860 RETURN
READY.
```

Figure 5.16: Program Listing: Four-Point Centered Average

LINEAR REGRESSION

Description

The linear regression technique allows you to find the "best" straight line for a set of data. The selected line is the one that best meets the regression criteria. You run the Linear Regression program by calling it from the program menu. It uses the data stored with the Input Data program. The program displays the equation for the straight line on your screen. You can also plot the straight line with the plot program, but the resulting plot will not appear straight because of the vertical resolution of the display.

Example

Frank has obtained data from an experiment and would like the equation for the best straight line for these data. The data are:

Point	1	2	3	4	5	6	7	8	9	10	11
Data	1	2	3	5	5	6	7	9	10	11	11

Point	12	13	14	15	16	17	18	19	20	21	22
Data	12	13	14	14	15	16	17	19	20	21	22

The screen display for this example appears in Figure 5.17. The program listing is shown in Figure 5.18.

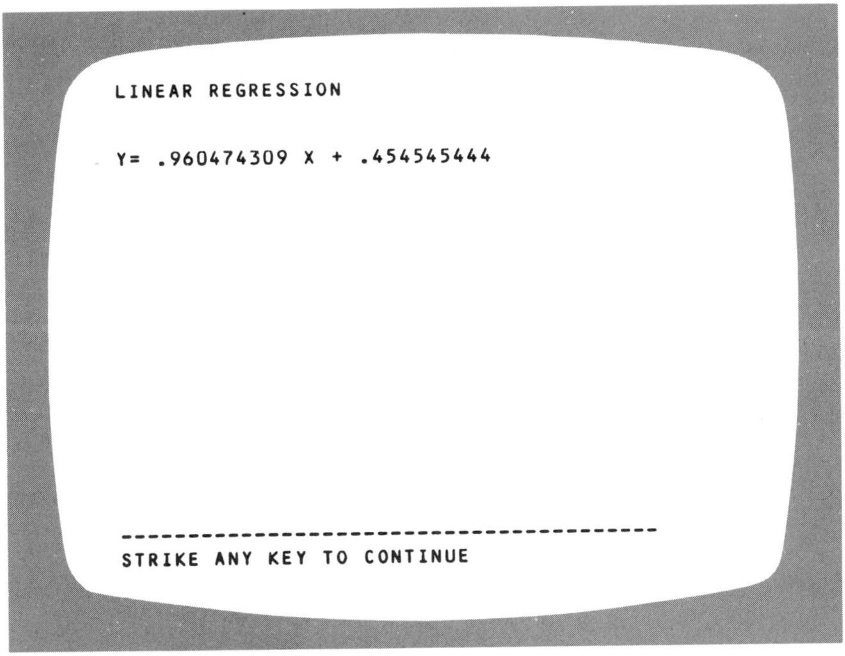

Figure 5.17: Screen Display: Linear Regression

```
1870 REM ------------------------------
1880 N$=        "LINEAR REGRESSION"
1890 REM ------------------------------
1900 GOSUB 6200: REM INITIALIZE
1910 SX=0:SY=0:XY=0:X2=0
1920 FOR I=1 TO ND
1930 SX=SX+I
1940 SY=SY+D(I)
1950 XY=XY+D(I)*I
1960 X2=X2+I^2
1970 NEXT I
1980 M=(XY-SX*SY/ND)/(X2-SX^2/ND)
1990 B=SY/ND-M*SX/ND
2000 PRINT
2010 PRINT"Y=";M;"X +";B
2020 REM UPDATE RESULT ARRAY
2030 FOR I=1 TO ND
2040 R(I)=M*I+B
2050 NEXT I
2060 GOSUB 7400
2070 RETURN
```

Figure 5.18: Program Listing: Linear Regression

6

RECORD KEEPING PROGRAMS

This chapter shows you how to use the diskette storage system to store, retrieve, and analyze data. We shall first create a personal file that you can use to store names and addresses. You can use the personal files you create for phone directories, business mailing lists, and other applications. Then we'll show you how to create an automobile file that will make it easy to keep mileage records for your car.

Disk file programs usually don't appear in collections of programs, because they can be very complicated. But by using our central subroutine library, we have been able to reduce the usual complexity of these disk file programs. The results are programs that are easy to enter and use.

Prior to using the programs in this chapter, you must add several new subroutines to the SUBLIB file. These subroutines begin at line numbers 3000 and 3800; the subroutine listings are in Appendix A.

Unlike the other chapters, the programs in this chapter must be saved in *two* files—one containing the Personal File programs and the other containing the Automobile File programs. Each set of programs begins with a menu.

These programs automatically create data files on your disk drive. You can add these files to your program disk, or you can use a freshly formatted disk.

First let's define a few terms. An *item* is the smallest quantity stored in a file. For the personal file the items are last name, first name, telephone number, street address, city, state, and zip code. The items in the auto record are date, odometer reading, and gallons of gas used. A *record* is defined as a set of items. For the personal file a record is the name, address, and phone number for each individual. Finally, a *file* is a set of records.

PERSONAL FILE MENU

The programs for the personal file run from a menu. As you can see, the individual programs allow you to add records, delete records, list the entire file, search for individual records in the file, and save your file on disks. You add records to your file with the Add Record program. The Delete Record program removes records from your file; you also change a record by deleting it and then reentering it with new information. The List File program displays the entire file on your screen. The Search Record program allows you to find all records with the same last name. The Save File program saves your file onto disk. You must use this program to be able to use your file at a later time. Figure 6.1 shows the menu screen display. Figure 6.2 shows the menu program listing.

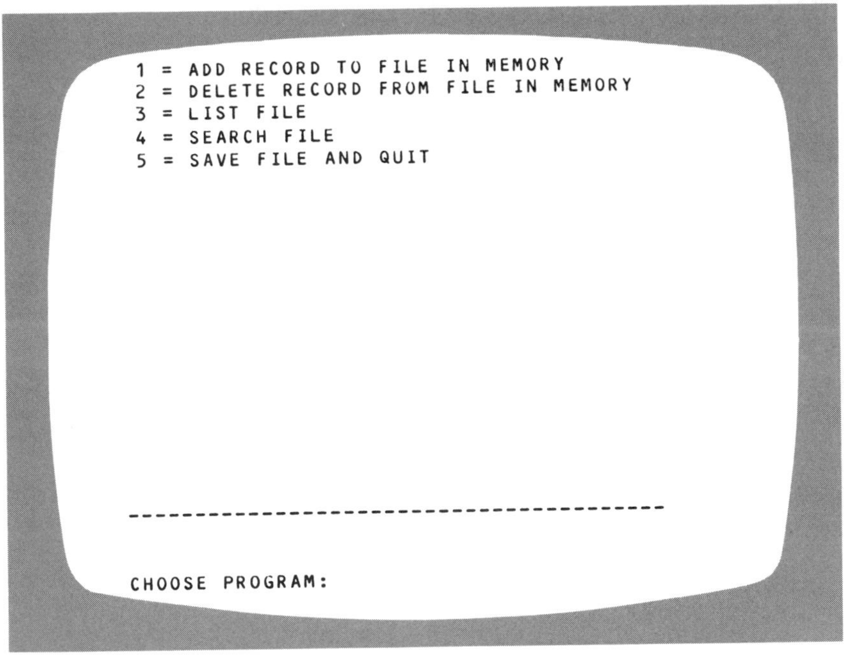

Figure 6.1: Screen Display: Personal File Menu

```
100 REM ------------------------------
110 N$=        "PERSONAL FILE"
120 REM ------------------------------
125 DIM P$(40,8)
126 FOR I=1 TO 40: FOR J=1 TO 8
127 P$(I,J)="A"
128 NEXT J: NEXT I
130 GOSUB 6200: REM INITIALIZE
132 F$="PERSONAL DATA"
135 GOSUB 1350: REM SPECIAL INITIALIZE
160 X$(1)="ADD RECORD TO FILE IN MEMORY"
170 X$(2)="DELETE RECORD FROM FILE IN MEMORY"
180 X$(3)="LIST FILE"
190 X$(4)="SEARCH FILE"
200 X$(5)="SAVE FILE AND QUIT"
220 N=5: GOSUB 7000: REM DISPLAY MENU
230 ON X GOSUB 650,810,980,1090,1270
240 GOTO 160
```

Figure 6.2: Program Listing: Personal File Menu

PERSONAL FILE SUBROUTINES

As you enter the menu program you should also enter the subroutines shown in Figure 6.3. The first routine is used by the List Personal File program to list your file on the screen. The Initialize File subroutine is used only once, when you first create your personal file. The first time you run the personal file program, the Initialize subroutine automatically creates an empty file on the disk. You then begin to fill in the file with the Add Record program, saving the file when you're done. The next time you use the program, the Initialize subroutine does nothing, because the file has already been created. The Load File subroutine loads the personal file you have saved into your computer's memory.

```
250 REM ------------------------------
260 REM LIST RECORD ON SCREEN
270 REM ------------------------------
280 PRINT L;". ";TAB(15);P$(L,1);", ";P$(L,2)
290 PRINT TAB(15);P$(L,3)
300 PRINT TAB(15);P$(L,4)
310 PRINT TAB(15);P$(L,5);", ";P$(L,6);" ";P$(L,7)
320 PRINT: RETURN
500 REM ------------------------------
510 N$=   "INITIALIZE FILE ON DISK"
520 REM ------------------------------
525 GOSUB 6200
530 OPEN 2,8,2,"0:PERSONAL DATA,SEQ,W"
540 PRINT# 2,0
545 FOR J=1TO8:PRINT# 2,"A": NEXT
550 CLOSE 2
560 RETURN
570 REM ------------------------------
580 N$=   "LOAD FILE IN FROM DISK"
590 REM ------------------------------
600 GOSUB 6200
610 REM CALL LOAD SUBROUTINE
620 GOSUB 3800
640 RETURN
```

Figure 6.3: Program Listing: Personal File Subroutines

ADD RECORD

Description

The Add Record program is the one you use to add information to your file. You run the program by displaying the Personal File Menu and depressing the 1 on your keyboard. You are asked to enter the information that will appear in your file: last name, first name, telephone number, street address, city, state, and zip code. Records are stored in the order in which they are added.

Example

Figure 6.4 shows a screen display for a typical Add Record dialog. Figure 6.5 shows the listing for the Add Record program.

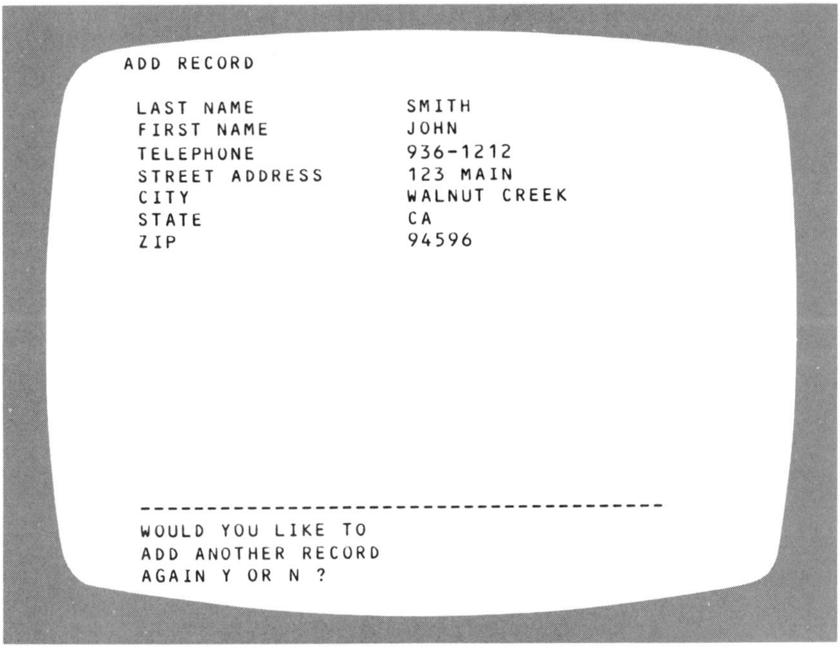

Figure 6.4: Screen Display: Add Record

```
650 REM ------------------------------
660 N$=          "ADD RECORD"
670 REM ------------------------------
680 GOSUB 6200: K=1: REM INITIALIZE
690 Q1$="ENTER DATA":Q2$=""
700 X=3: Y=2:NR=NR+1
710 Q3$="LAST NAME":GOSUB 5000: INPUT P$(NR,1)
715 X=1: Y=3:GOSUB 4200:PRINT Q3$,,P$(NR,1)
720 Q3$="FIRST NAME":GOSUB 5000: INPUT P$(NR,2)
725 Y=4:GOSUB 4200:PRINT Q3$,P$(NR,2)
730 Q3$="TELEPHONE":GOSUB 5000: INPUT P$(NR,3)
735 Y=5:GOSUB 4200:PRINT Q3$,,P$(NR,3)
740 Q3$="STREET ADDRESS":GOSUB 5000: INPUT P$(NR,4)
745 Y=6:GOSUB 4200:PRINT Q3$,P$(NR,4)
750 Q3$="CIT Y":GOSUB 5000:INPUT P$(NR,5)
755 Y=7:GOSUB 4200: PRINT Q3$,,P$(NR,5)
760 Q3$="STATE":GOSUB 5000:INPUT P$(NR,6)
765 Y=8:GOSUB 4200:PRINT Q3$,,P$(NR,6)
770 Q3$="ZIP":GOSUB 5000: INPUT P$(NR,7)
775 Y=9:GOSUB 4200: PRINT Q3$,,P$(NR,7)
780 Q2$="ADD ANOTHER RECORD": GOSUB 3400
790 IF YN$="N" THEN RETURN
800 GOTO 650
```

Figure 6.5: Program Listing: Add Record

DELETE RECORD

Description

This program is used to delete old information from your personal file. You can correct information by first deleting it with the Delete Record program and then reentering correct data with the Add Record program. You use this program by indicating the number of the record you wish to delete. All subsequent records are renumbered so that the numbering remains consecutive. You can obtain the record number from the List Personal File program or the Search Personal File program. Figure 6.6 is the Delete Record program listing.

```
810 REM ------------------------------
820 N$=     "DELETE RECORD FROM FILE"
830 REM ------------------------------
840 GOSUB 6200
850 Q1$="NUMBER OF RECORD TO DELETE"
860 Q2$="":Q3$="": GOSUB 5000
870 INPUT R
880 IF R>=1 AND R<=NR THEN 910
890 X=1: Y=18: GOSUB 4200
900 PRINT"RECORD NOT FOUND":GOTO 950
910 IF R=NR THEN NR=NR-1: GOTO 950
920 FOR I=R TO NR-1
930 FOR J=1 TO 8
935 P$(I,J)=P$(I+1,J)
940 NEXT J: NEXT I: NR=NR-1
950 Q2$="DELETE A RECORD": GOSUB 3400
960 IF YN$="N" THEN RETURN
970 GOTO810
```

Figure 6.6: Program Listing: Delete Record

LIST PERSONAL FILE

Description

This program lists your personal file. You run the program by activating the Personal File Menu program and depressing the 3 on your keyboard. Each record in the file is displayed on your screen. Records will scroll on the screen.

Example

Figure 6.7 shows a screen display of a personal file. Note that each record has a record number and that blank lines separate individual records. You will use the record number when you delete records from the file. Figure 6.8 displays the program listing for the List Personal File program.

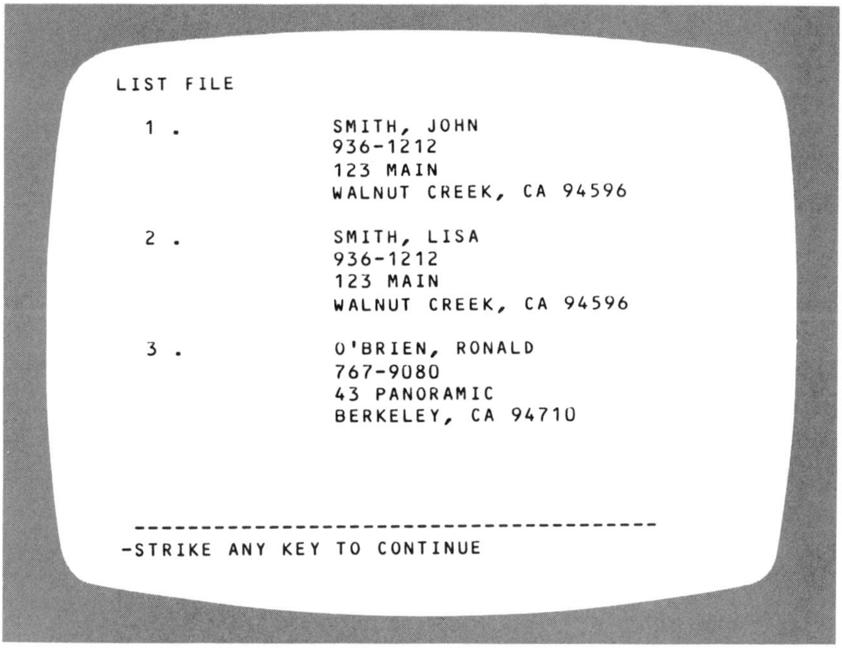

Figure 6.7: Screen Display: List Personal File

```
980 REM ------------------------------
990 N$=          "LIST FILE"
1000 REM------------------------------
1010 GOSUB 6200
1015 IF NR=0 THEN GOSUB 7400:RETURN
1020 FOR L=1 TO NR
1030 GOSUB 250
1040 FOR X=1 TO 1000: NEXT X
1050 NEXT L
1060 PRINT: PRINT: PRINT: PRINT
1070 GOSUB 7400: REM PAUSE
1080 RETURN
```

Figure 6.8: Program Listing: List Personal File

SEARCH PERSONAL FILE

Description

The Search Personal File program allows you to find an individual record without listing the entire file. You enter the last name of the individual you are searching for. The first record having the same last name you specify is displayed on your screen. The program then asks if you would like to search for additional matches. The program tells you if no last name matches are found.

The spelling you specify must match exactly the spelling in your file. Therefore, you must be consistent in the way you add records to your file. If you enter DU BOIS as the last name in your record and you search for the name DUBOIS, the program will tell you that no match is found.

Example

Let's search for the record for RONALD O'BRIEN. The screen display is shown in Figure 6.9. Figure 6.10 is the Search Personal File program listing.

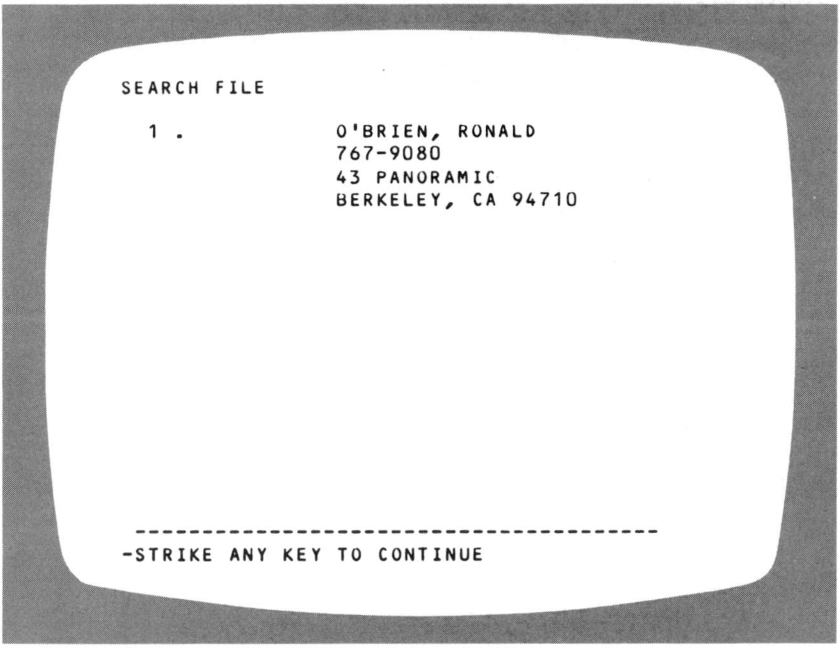

Figure 6.9: Screen Display: Search Personal File

```
1090 REM ----------------------------
1100 N$=          "SEARCH FILE"
1110 REM ----------------------------
1120 GOSUB 6200
1130 Q1$="SEARCH FOR LAST NAME:"
1140 Q2$="": Q3$="LAST NAME: "
1150 GOSUB 5000: INPUT NA$
1160 F=0:X=1: Y=3:GOSUB 4200
1170 FOR I=1 TO NR
1180 IF NA$<>P$(I,1) THEN 1210
1185 GOSUB 6200
1190 F=1: L=I: GOSUB 250
1200 GOSUB 7400
1210 NEXT I
1220 X=1: Y=18: GOSUB 4200
1230 IF F=0 THEN PRINT"NO MATCHES FOUND"
1240 Q2$="SEARCH": GOSUB 3400
1250 IF YN$="N" THEN RETURN
1260 GOTO 1090
```

Figure 6.10: Program Listing: Search Personal File

SAVE FILE

As you worked on it, your entire file was stored in your computer's memory. You may want to use it at another time. If so, you must save it onto disk when you are done working on it. The Save File program, shown in Figure 6.11, will accomplish this.

```
1270 REM -----------------------------
1280 N$=      "SAVE FILE TO DISK"
1290 REM -----------------------------
1300 GOSUB 6200
1310 REM CALL SAVE SUBROUTINE
1320 GOSUB 3000
1330 PRINT"OK FILE SAVED" : PRINT
1340 END
1350 REM-------------------------------
1360 REM SPECIAL INITIALIZING ROUTINE
1370 REM
1380 REM LOADS IN FILE FROM DISK, OR
1390 REM IF NONE EXISTS, CREATES ONE
1400 REM
1410 REM-------------------------------
1420 OPEN 15,8,15: REM OPEN ERROR CHANNEL
1430 A$="0:"+F$+",SEQ,R"
1440 OPEN 3,8,3,A$
1450 INPUT# 3,A
1460 INPUT# 15,E,A$,B$,C$
1470 CLOSE 3
1475 IF E<>0 THEN PRINT# 15,"I"
1480 CLOSE 15
1490 NR=0
1500 IF E=0 THEN GOSUB 570
1510 IF E=62 THEN GOSUB 500
1520 IF E=0 OR E=62 THEN RETURN
1530 PRINT"ERROR # ";E
1540 END
```

Figure 6.11: Program Listing: Save File

AUTOMOBILE FILE MENU

We will now develop a disk file that keeps mileage records for your automobile. You can use these programs to enter a calendar date, odometer reading, and amount of gasoline purchased. The List Automobile File program computes the average miles per gallon and returns that figure in the listing. When you are through adding a record or set of records to your file, you must save the file onto disk with the Save File program to maintain a complete record of your car's mileage. You call the Automobile Record programs from a menu program. Figure 6.12 shows the screen display for the Automobile Record Menu. Figure 6.13 is the menu program listing.

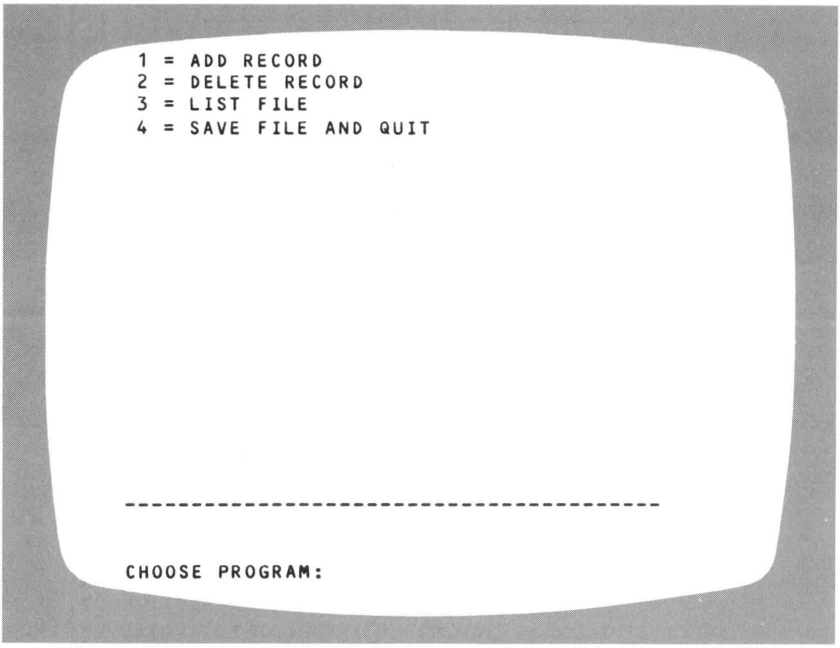

Figure 6.12: Screen Display: Automobile Record Menu

```
100 REM ------------------------------
110 N$=        "AUTOMOBILE FILE"
120 REM ------------------------------
130 DIM P$(40,8)
140 FOR I=1 TO 40
150 FOR J=1 TO 8
160 P$(I,J)="A"
170 NEXT J: NEXT I
175 F$="AUTOMOBILE DATA"
180 GOSUB 6200: REM INITIALIZE
185 GOSUB 1000:REM  SPECIAL INITIALIZE ROUTINE
210 X$(1)="ADD RECORD"
220 X$(2)="DELETE RECORD"
230 X$(3)="LIST FILE"
240 X$(4)="SAVE FILE AND QUIT"
260 N=4: GOSUB 7000: REM MENU
270 ON X GOSUB 450,570,770,920
280 GOTO 210
```

Figure 6.13: Program Listing: Automobile Record Menu

AUTOMOBILE FILE SUBROUTINES

As you enter the menu program you should also enter the subroutines shown in Figure 6.14. The Initialize subroutine is used only once, when you first create your automobile file. The first time you run the automobile file program, the Initialize subroutine automatically creates an empty file on the disk. You then begin to fill in the file with the Add Record program, saving the file when you're done. The next time you use the program, the Initialize subroutine does nothing, because the file has already been created. The Load File subroutine loads the automobile file you have saved into your computer's memory.

```
290 REM -----------------------------
300 N$=    "INITIALIZE FILE ON DISK"
310 REM -----------------------------
320 GOSUB 6200: REM INITIALIZE
330 OPEN 2,8,2,"0:AUTOMOBILE DATA,SEQ,W"
340 PRINT# 2,0
345 FOR J=1 TO 8: PRINT#2,"A": NEXT
350 CLOSE 2
360 RETURN
370 REM -----------------------------
380 N$=    "LOAD FILE IN FROM DISK"
390 REM -----------------------------
400 GOSUB 6200: REM INITIALIZE
410 REM CALL LOAD FILE ROUTINE
420 GOSUB 3800
440 RETURN
```

Figure 6.14: Automobile File Subroutines

ADD RECORD

Description

You use the Add Record program to add records to your automobile file. You enter the date, odometer reading, and gallons of gasoline purchased. Again, records are stored in the order in which they are added. If you make an error as you create a record, the average miles per gallon may be incorrectly computed. You should check your records carefully immediately after you enter them, because an incorrect record is difficult to correct once you have added other records.

Example

On February 17, 1982, you purchase 14.9 gallons of gas with an odometer reading of 13,523 miles. Figure 6.15 shows the screen display as you add this information to the file. Figure 6.16 is the program listing for the Add Record program.

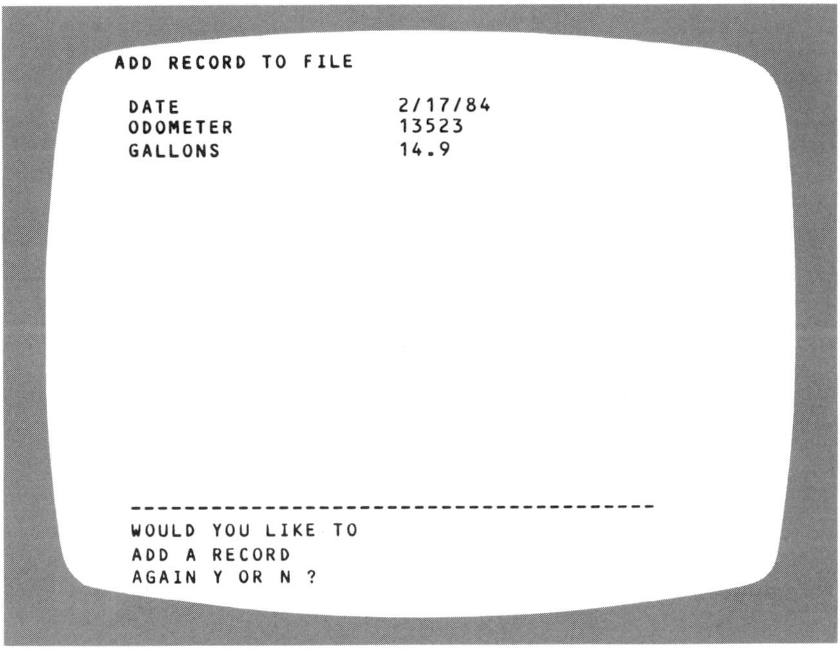

Figure 6.15: Screen Display: Add Record

```
450 REM ------------------------------
460 N$=      "ADD RECORD TO FILE"
470 REM ------------------------------
480 GOSUB 6200
490 Q1$="ENTER DATA":Q2$=""
500 NR=NR+1
510 Q3$="DATE":GOSUB 5000: INPUT P$(NR,1)
515 X=1: Y=3:GOSUB 4200: PRINT Q3$,,P$(NR,1)
520 Q3$="ODOMETER":GOSUB 5000: INPUT P$(NR,2)
525 Y=4:GOSUB 4200: PRINT Q3$,,P$(NR,2)
530 Q3$="GALLONS": GOSUB 5000: INPUT P$(NR,3)
535 Y=5:GOSUB 4200: PRINT Q3$,,P$(NR,3)
540 Q2$="ADD A RECORD": GOSUB 3400
550 IF YN$="N" THEN RETURN
560 GOTO 450
```

Figure 6.16: Program Listing: Add Record

DELETE RECORD

The Delete Record program allows you to delete a record from your file. You can use this program to delete information that you enter incorrectly. You delete a record by specifying its number. When you delete a record in the middle of a file, all subsequent records are renumbered so that there are no holes in the file. Figure 6.17 shows the Delete Record program listing. You must delete records immediately upon incorrect entry; otherwise, the program will incorrectly compute miles per gallon.

```
570 REM -----------------------------
580 N$=        "DELETE A RECORD"
590 REM -----------------------------
600 GOSUB 6200: REM INITIALIZE
610 Q1$="NUMBER OF RECORD TO DELETE:"
620 Q2$="":Q3$=""
630 GOSUB 5000: INPUT R: REM GET RECORD #
640 NR=NR-1
650 IF R=NR+1 THEN 740
660 IF R>=1 AND R<=NR THEN 690
670 X=1: Y=18:GOSUB 4200: REM LOCATE
680 NR=NR+1:PRINT"RECORD NOT FOUND": GOTO 740
690 FOR I=R TO NR
700 FOR J=1 TO 3
710 P$(I,J)=P$(I+1,J)
720 NEXT J
730 NEXT I
740 Q2$="DELETE A RECORD": GOSUB 3400
750 IF YN$="N" THEN RETURN
760 GOTO 570
```

Figure 6.17: Program Listing: Delete Record

LIST AUTOMOBILE FILE

Description

The List Automobile File program lists the contents of your automobile record on your screen. This program also computes and displays the average miles per gallon for each record. The screen will scroll slowly enough for you to read the information.

You can easily monitor your car's performance with this program. A sudden drop in average miles per gallon may indicate a problem with your car.

Example

You would like to view the contents of your automobile log. Figure 6.18 is the screen display for this example. Figure 6.19 is the List Automobile File program listing.

```
LIST FILE

 NO. DATE       MILES     GAL      AVERAGE
  1  1/31/84    12730     15.6
  2  2/7/84     12925     13.1     14.89
  3  2/12/84    13210     15.8     18.04
  4  2/17/84    13523     14.9     21.01
  5  2/22/84    13801     15.2     18.29

 ----------------------------------------
 STRIKE ANY KEY TO CONTINUE
```

Figure 6.18: Screen Display: List Automobile File

```
770 REM ------------------------------
780 N$=          "LIST FILE"
790 REM ------------------------------
800 GOSUB 6200: REM INITIALIZE
810 PRINT"NO. DATE      MILES     GAL     AVERAGE"
815 IF NR=0 THEN GOSUB 7400: RETURN
820 FOR I=1 TO NR
830 PRINT I;TAB(4);P$(I,1);TAB(14);
840 PRINT P$(I,2);TAB(24);P$(I,3);TAB(31);
850 IF I=1 THEN PRINT: GOTO 890
860 M=VAL(P$(I,2))-VAL(P$(I-1,2)): G=VAL(P$(I,3))
870 DC=M/G+.005-INT(M/G): DC$=STR$(DC)
875 DP$=MID$(DC$,2,3): IN$=STR$(INT(M/G))
880 PRINT IN$+DP$: REM ROUNDED AVERAGE
885 FOR J=1 TO 200: NEXT J: REM DELAY
890 NEXT I
900 GOSUB 7400: REM PAUSE
910 RETURN
```

Figure 6.19: Program Listing: List Automobile File

SAVE FILE

Up to this point your file has been maintained in the computer's memory. If you want a complete record of your car's mileage, you must use the Save File program to save your file onto disk. The Save File program is shown in Figure 6.20.

```
920 REM ------------------------------
930 N$=      "SAVE FILE TO DISK"
940 REM ------------------------------
950 GOSUB 6200: REM INITIALIZE
960 REM CALL SAVE SUBROUTINE
970 GOSUB 3000
980 PRINT"OK FILE SAVED":PRINT
990 END
1000 REM ----------------------------
1010 REM   SPECIAL INITIALIZE ROUTINE
1020 REM
1030 REM LOADS FILE IN FROM DISK, OR
1040 REM IF NONE EXISTS, CREATES ONE
1050 REM
1060 REM ----------------------------
1065 NR=0
1070 OPEN 15,8,15:REM OPEN COMMAND CHANNEL
1080 A$="0:"+F$+",SEQ,R"
1090 OPEN 3,8,3,A$
1100 INPUT# 3,A
1110 INPUT#15,E,A$,B$,C$
1120 CLOSE 3
1130 IF E<>0 THEN PRINT#15,"I"
1140 CLOSE 15
1150 IF E=0 THEN GOSUB 370: RETURN
1160 IF E=62 THEN GOSUB 290: RETURN
1170 PRINT" ERROR# ";E
1180 END
```

Figure 6.20: Program Listing: Save File

7

MATHEMATICS PRACTICE PROGRAMS

This chapter presents three sets of programs that allow you to use your computer to practice arithmetic. You must save each set in its own file. Each set runs from a menu, which you enter first. We provide drills in addition, subtraction, multiplication, and division, with both whole numbers and fractions. The three menus provide programs at multiple levels of difficulty; the programs are suitable for students from elementary to high school level. Each program keeps track of right and wrong answers. You will find that these programs can greatly sharpen your math skills; they are also helpful in completing homework assignments!

MATHEMATICS PRACTICE I MENU

The first set of four programs provides practice in adding, subtracting, multiplying, and dividing two whole numbers. You begin this set of programs by displaying the Mathematics Practice I Menu. Depress a number key to choose the drill you want. Once you have chosen the drill, the program asks you to choose the largest number you want to work with. Then the program presents you with two numbers and an operator to indicate addition, subtraction, multiplication, or division. You enter your answer from left to right. Each program keeps track of the total number of correct and incorrect answers. (Be sure to challenge yourself by choosing a large number!)

To use these programs you first enter the menu program and two common subroutines. Figure 7.1 shows the screen display for the menu program. Figure 7.2 is the program listing of the menu program.

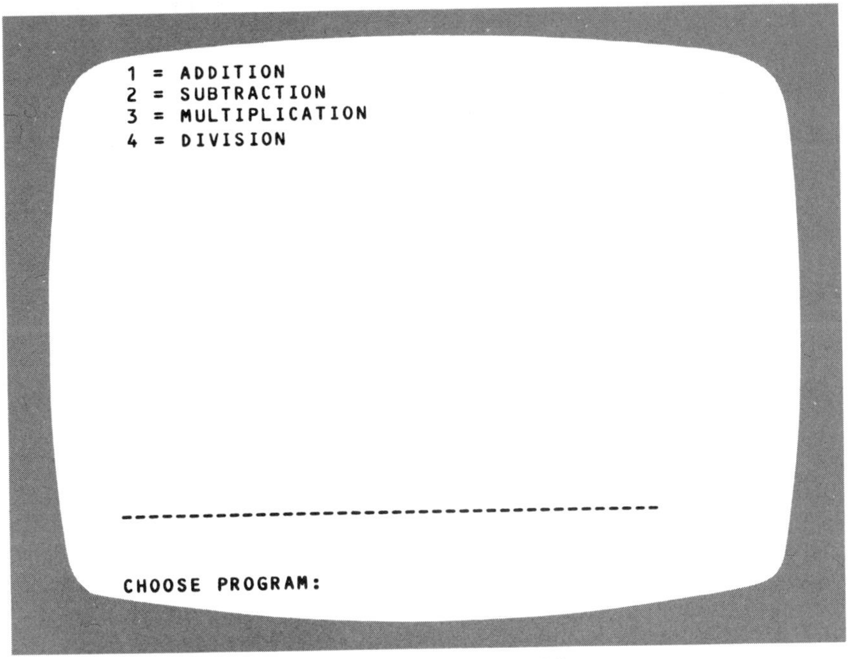

Figure 7.1: Screen Display: Mathematics Practice I Menu

```
100 REM --------------------------------
110 N$=     "MATHEMATICS PRACTICE I"
120 REM --------------------------------
130 GOSUB 6200: REM INITIALIZE
140 X$(1)="ADDITION"
150 X$(2)="SUBTRACTION"
160 X$(3)="MULTIPLICATION"
170 X$(4)="DIVISION"
180 N=4: GOSUB 7000: REM DISPLAY MENU
190 R=0:W=0:P=X
200 Q1$="WHAT IS THE LARGEST NUMBER"
210 Q2$="YOU WOULD LIKE TO"
220 Q3$="PRACTICE WITH"
230 GOSUB 5000: REM ASK QUESTIONS
240 PRINT TAB(22);: INPUT L
250 ON P GOSUB 490,620,770,900
260 GOTO 100
```

Figure 7.2: Program Listing: Mathematics Practice I Menu

MATHEMATICS PRACTICE I SUBROUTINES

The Mathematics Practice I programs use two subroutines to display the questions and print and tabulate the answers. You must enter them before you enter the actual drills. We use these subroutines to greatly shorten the programs that follow. The subroutines generate problems with a random number generator, and keep track of the total problems done and the total number of correct and incorrect answers. The subroutines are listed in Figure 7.3.

```
280 REM ------------------------------
290 REM DISPLAY QUESTION AND GET ANSWER
300 REM ------------------------------
310 X=21: Y=5:GOSUB 4200: REM LOCATE
320 S=4-LEN(STR$(N1)): PRINT SPC(S);N1
330 S=4-LEN(STR$(N2)): PRINT TAB(19);SN$;SPC(S);N2
340 PRINT TAB(20);"----":PRINT
350 INPUT"TYPE ANSWER        ";P
360 X=1: Y=8:GOSUB 4200: REM LOCATE
370 PRINT"CORRECT ANSWER IS:  ";
375 RETURN
380 REM ------------------------------
390 REM        FINISH THE PROBLEM
400 REM ------------------------------
410 PRINT:PRINT:PRINT"YOU ARE ";
420 IF S=1 THEN PRINT"RIGHT":R=R+1
430 IF S=0 THEN PRINT"WRONG":W=W+1
440 PRINT"PROBLEMS DONE";TAB(19);R+W
450 PRINT"CORRECT";TAB(19);R
460 PRINT"ERRORS";TAB(19);W
470 Q2$="PRACTICE": GOSUB 3400: REM ASK FOR ANOTHER
480 RETURN
```

Figure 7.3: Program Listing: Mathematics Practice I Subroutines

ADDITION

Description

The addition drill presents two random numbers at a time. You must enter the answer from left to right, which will sometimes mean that you must first work out the problem on a piece of paper. The program selects the largest number you work with from the answer you enter when the menu first appears.

Example

The sample display in Figure 7.4 shows an incorrect addition. Note that six problems have been done; four out of six answers have been correct. The Addition program is listed in Figure 7.5.

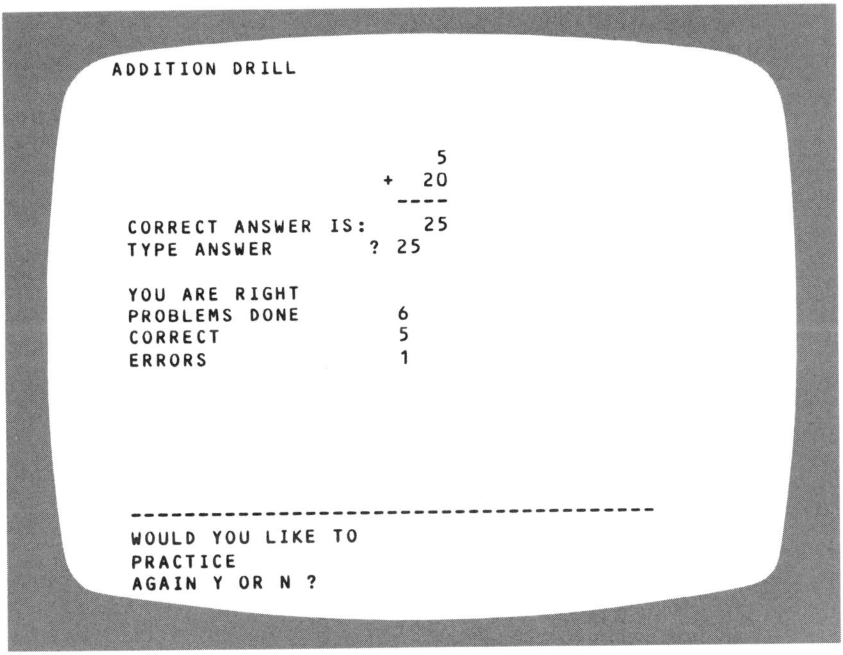

Figure 7.4: Screen Display: Addition

```
490 REM -------------------------------
500 N$=        "ADDITION DRILL"
510 REM -------------------------------
520 GOSUB 6200: REM INITIALIZE
530 N1=INT(RND(0)*L)
540 N2=INT(RND(0)*L)
550 SN$="+"
560 GOSUB 280: REM DISP QUEST, GET ANS
570 S=0: IF P=N1+N2 THEN S=1
580 U=4-LEN(STR$(N1+N2)): PRINT SPC(U);N1+N2
590 GOSUB 380: REM FINISH UP
600 IF YN$="N" THEN RETURN
610 GOTO 490
```

Figure 7.5: Program Listing: Addition

SUBTRACTION

Description

The subtraction drill is similar to the addition drill. The program's selection method for the two numbers guarantees that a positive answer always results. Remember, practice makes perfect—keep trying with new problems.

Example

The screen display in Figure 7.6 shows an incorrect subtraction. Note that two out of three problems have been correctly answered. Figure 7.7 displays the program listing for the subtraction drill.

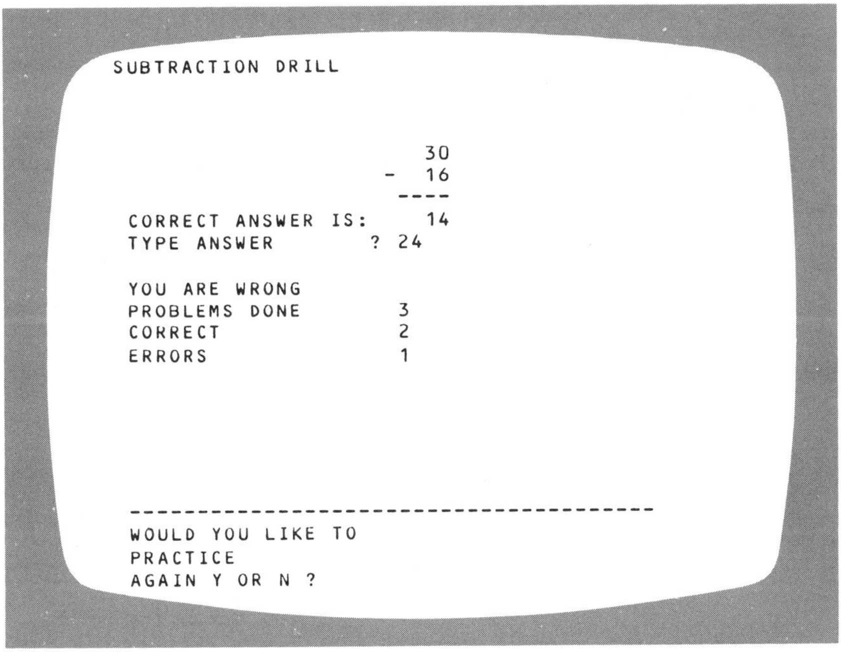

Figure 7.6: Screen Display: Subtraction

```
620 REM --------------------------------
630 N$=      "SUBTRACTION DRILL"
640 REM --------------------------------
650 GOSUB 6200: REM INITIALIZE
660 N1=INT(RND(0)*L)
670 N2=INT(RND(0)*L)
680 N3=N1: IF N1>N2 GOTO 700
690 N1=N2: N2=N3
700 SN$="-"
710 GOSUB 280: REM DISP QUEST, GET ANS
720 S=0: IF P=N1-N2 THEN S=1
730 U=4-LEN(STR$(N1-N2)): PRINT SPC(U);N1-N2
740 GOSUB 380: REM FINISH UP
750 IF YN$="N" THEN RETURN
760 GOTO 620
```

Figure 7.7: Program Listing: Subtraction

MULTIPLICATION

Description

This program allows you to practice multiplying two numbers. The program generates random numbers; you choose the largest number you want to work with at the time you select the multiplication drill from the menu. This program displays the answer on a single line. If you are multiplying by two or more digits, you may wish to use the Long Multiplication program, which appears later in this chapter. The Long Multiplication program displays the intermediate steps necessary to compute the answer.

Example

Figure 7.8 shows a screen display for the Multiplication program. This display shows that four out of five problems have been done correctly. Figure 7.9 is the program listing for the multiplication drill.

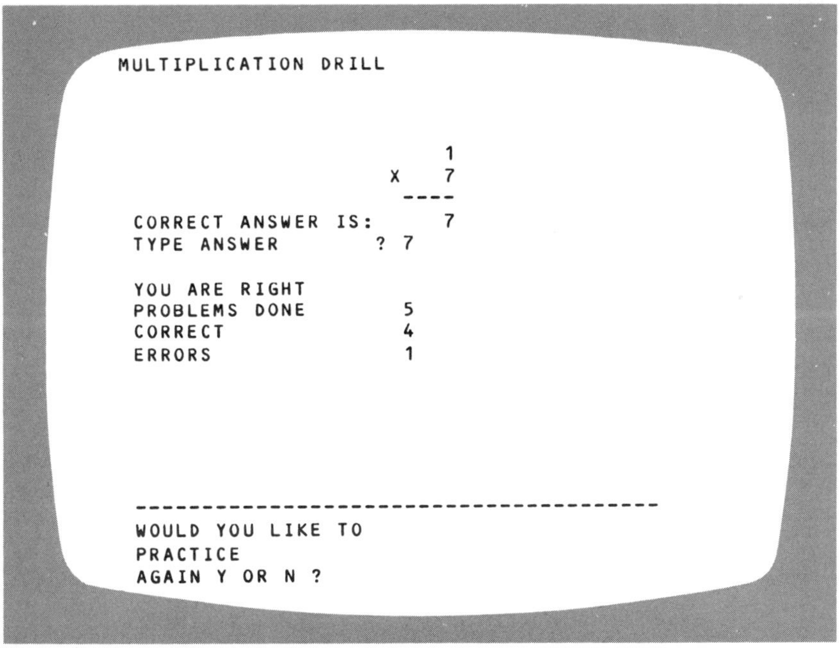

Figure 7.8: Screen Display: Multiplication

```
770 REM ------------------------------
780 N$=    "MULTIPLICATION DRILL"
790 REM ------------------------------
800 GOSUB 6200
810 N1=INT(RND(0)*L)
820 N2=INT(RND(0)*L)
830 SN$="X"
840 GOSUB 280: REM DISP QUEST, GET ANS
850 S=0: IF P=N1*N2 THEN S=1
860 U=4-LEN(STR$(N1*N2)):PRINT SPC(U);N1*N2
870 GOSUB 380: REM FINISH UP
880 IF YN$="N" THEN RETURN
890 GOTO 770
```

Figure 7.9: Program Listing: Multiplication

DIVISION

Description

The fourth mathematics drill allows you to practice dividing two whole numbers. Again, you choose the largest number you want to divide by (the denominator) when the Division program is selected from the Mathematics Practice I Menu. The program generates numbers which guarantee that a whole number results from your division. Note that the largest number you work with is the largest answer in this program.

Example

Figure 7.10 shows a screen display for the Division program. Note that this is the fifth problem completed, and that all the answers have been correct. The listing for the Division program appears in Figure 7.11.

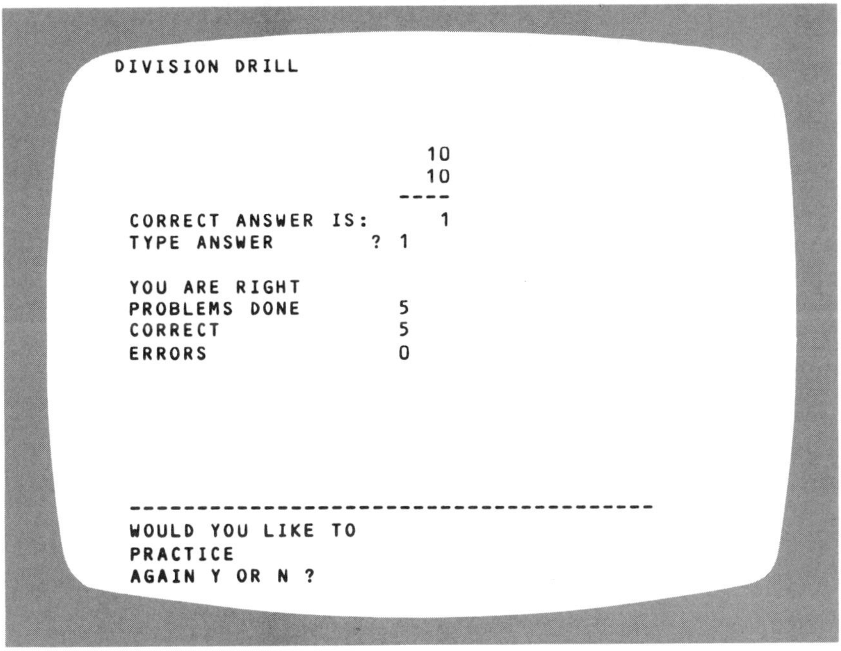

Figure 7.10: Screen Display: Division

```
900 REM ------------------------------
910 N$=       "DIVISION DRILL"
920 REM ------------------------------
930 GOSUB 6200
940 N1=INT(RND(0)*L)
950 N2=INT(RND(0)*L): IF N2=0 THEN 950
960 N1=N1*N2
970 SN$="/"
980 GOSUB 280: REM DISP QUEST, GET ANS
990 S=0: IF P=N1/N2 THEN S=1
1000 U=4-LEN(STR$(N1/N2)): PRINT SPC(U);N1/N2
1010 GOSUB 380: REM FINISH UP
1020 IF YN$="N" THEN RETURN
1030 GOTO 900
```

Figure 7.11: Program Listing: Division

MATHEMATICS PRACTICE II MENU

Mathematics Practice II consists of two advanced mathematics drills. The first program allows you to practice adding numbers in columns. The second program allows you to practice multiplying large numbers using long multiplication. For both programs, work out the answer with pencil and paper and then enter it into the computer. Note that the Multiplication program provides all intermediate steps. Figure 7.12 is a screen display of the Mathematics Practice II menu. Figure 7.13 is a listing of the menu program.

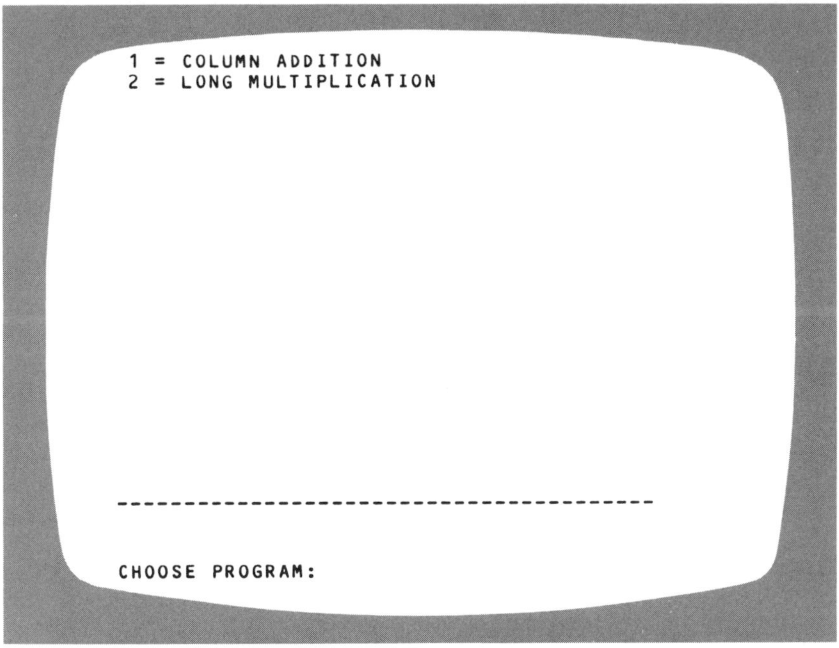

Figure 7.12: Screen Display: Mathematics Practice II Menu

```
100 REM ------------------------------
110 N$=   "MATHEMATICS PRACTICE II"
120 REM ------------------------------
130 GOSUB 6200: REM INITIALIZE
140 X$(1)="COLUMN ADDITION"
150 X$(2)="LONG MULTIPLICATION"
160 REM SET UP MENU AND DISPLAY IT
170 N=2: GOSUB 7000: REM DISPLAY MENU
180 ON X GOSUB 200,540
190 GOTO 100
```

Figure 7.13: Program Listing: Mathematics Practice II Menu

COLUMN ADDITION

Description

The Column Addition program allows you to practice adding columns of numbers. You select this drill by depressing the number 1 from the menu program. The program then asks you to enter both the largest number and how many numbers you would like to add. The program keeps track of correct and incorrect answers.

Example

Figure 7.14 shows the correct addition of five numbers. Figure 7.15 is the program listing for this mathematics drill.

```
200 REM ------------------------------
210 N$=        "COLUMN ADDITION"
220 REM ------------------------------
230 GOSUB 6200: REM INITIALIZE
240 Q1$=""
250 Q2$="WHAT IS THE LARGEST NUMBER"
260 Q3$="YOU WOULD LIKE TO ADD"
270 GOSUB 5000
280 INPUT LG: REM GET NUMBER
290 Q2$="HOW MANY NUMBERS"
300 GOSUB 5000
310 INPUT NU
320 R=0:W=0
330 GOSUB 6200: T=0
```

Figure 7.15: Program Listing: Column Addition (continues)

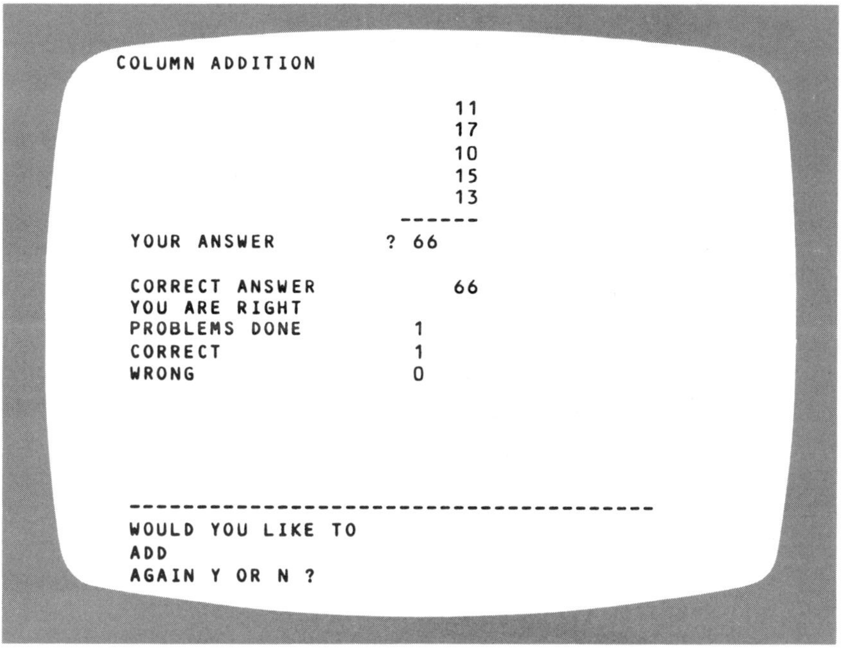

Figure 7.14: Screen Display: Column Addition

```
340 FOR I=1 TO NU
350 N1=INT(RND(0)*LG)
360 T=T+N1
370 S=6-LEN(STR$(N1))
380 PRINT TAB(20);SPC(S);N1
390 NEXT I
400 PRINT TAB(20);"------"
410 INPUT"YOUR ANSWER         ";A
420 PRINT
430 S=6-LEN(STR$(T))
440 PRINT"CORRECT ANSWER";TAB(20);SPC(S);T
450 PRINT"YOU ARE ";
460 IF T=A THEN PRINT"RIGHT":R=R+1
470 IF T<>A THEN PRINT"WRONG":W=W+1
480 PRINT"PROBLEMS DONE";TAB(20);R+W
490 PRINT"CORRECT";TAB(20);R
500 PRINT"WRONG";TAB(20);W
510 Q2$="ADD":GOSUB 3400: REM ASK FOR ANOTHER
520 IF YN$="N" THEN RETURN
530 GOTO 330
```

Figure 7.15: Program Listing: Column Addition

LONG MULTIPLICATION

Description

We now present a program that allows you to practice multiplying numbers using long multiplication. You select this program from the Mathematics Practice II Menu by pressing the 2 on your keyboard. You then enter the number of digits you wish to work with. The program presents you with two numbers to multiply; you work out your answer by hand and enter the final answer. The screen displays the correct answer and the steps that are necessary to compute the answer. By reviewing the various steps, you can see exactly where you make your mistakes.

Example

Figure 7.16 shows the result of multiplying two large numbers. Note that all of the intermediate results are displayed. Figure 7.17 is the Long Multiplication program listing.

```
540 REM -----------------------------
550 N$=     "LONG MULTIPLICATION"
560 REM -----------------------------
570 GOSUB 6200:: REM INITIALIZE
580 Q1$=""
590 Q2$="HOW MANY DIGITS"
600 Q3$="WOULD YOU LIKE TO MULTIPLY"
610 GOSUB 5000: REM GET NUMBER
620 INPUT N
630 GOSUB 6200
640 N1=0:N2=0
650 FOR I=0 TO N-1
660 N1(I)=INT(RND(0)*10): N1=N1+N1(I)*10^I
```

Figure 7.17: Program Listing: Long Multiplication (continues)

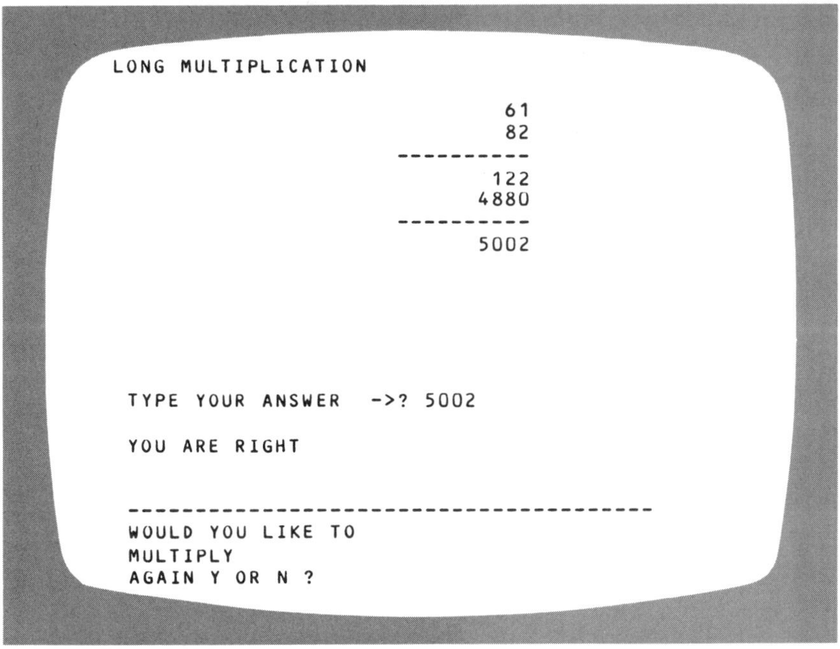

Figure 7.16: Screen Display: Long Multiplication

```
670 N2(I)=INT(RND(0)*10): N2=N2+N2(I)*10^I
680 NEXT I
690 S=10-LEN(STR$(N1)): PRINT TAB(20);SPC(S);N1
700 S=10-LEN(STR$(N2)): PRINT TAB(20);SPC(S);N2
710 PRINT TAB(20);"----------"
720 X=1: Y=16: GOSUB 4200
730 INPUT"TYPE YOUR ANSWER  ->";P
740 X=1: Y=6: GOSUB 4200
750 FOR I=0 TO N-1
760 A=N1*N2(I)*10^I:S=10-LEN(STR$(A))
770 PRINT TAB(20);SPC(S);A
780 NEXT I
790 PRINT TAB(20);"----------"
800 S=10-LEN(STR$(N1*N2)):PRINT TAB(20);SPC(S);N1*N2
810 X=1: Y=18: GOSUB 4200
820 IF P=N1*N2 THEN PRINT"YOU ARE RIGHT"
830 IF P<>N1*N2 THEN PRINT"YOU ARE WRONG"
840 Q2$="MULTIPLY": GOSUB 3400
850 IF YN$="N" THEN RETURN
860 GOTO 630
```

Figure 7.17: Program Listing: Long Multiplication

MATHEMATICS PRACTICE III MENU

The final set of mathematics drills allows you to practice adding, subtracting, multiplying, and dividing fractions. You work out your answers by hand and enter the final answer. All answers in this section are reduced to least-common-denominator form; conversions to mixed numbers are not made. Each program keeps track of your correct and incorrect answers.

The four fraction programs work from a common menu. Figure 7.18 displays the Mathematics Practice III Menu; Figure 7.19 is the listing of the menu program.

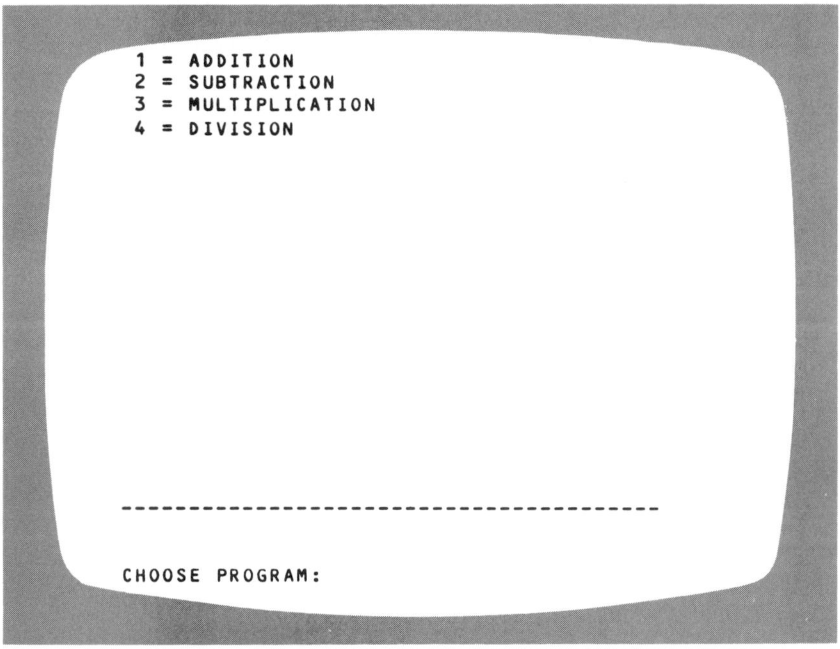

Figure 7.18: Screen Display: Mathematics Practice III Menu

```
100 REM ------------------------------
110 N$=    "MATHEMATICS PRACTICE III"
120 REM ------------------------------
130 GOSUB 6200: REM INITIALIZE
140 X$(1)="ADDITION"
150 X$(2)="SUBTRACTION"
160 X$(3)="MULTIPLICATION"
170 X$(4)="DIVISION"
180 N=4: GOSUB 7000: REM DISPLAY MENU
190 R=0: W=0: P=X
200 Q1$=""
210 Q2$="WHAT IS THE LARGEST DENOMINATOR"
220 Q3$="YOU WOULD LIKE TO PRACTICE WITH"
230 GOSUB 5000: INPUT LG
240 ON P GOSUB 810,960,1120,1260
250 GOTO 100
```

Figure 7.19: Program Listing: Mathematics Practice III Menu

FRACTION SUBROUTINES

Prior to entering the fraction programs, you should enter the four subroutines shown in Figure 7.20. These subroutines generate the fractions and the greatest common denominator, display the question, and print the answer.

The subroutines use a random number generator to select the numerators and denominators. They also display the problem on the screen in fraction form, as shown below:

$$\frac{4}{5} + \frac{5}{6}$$

When you answer, the subroutines ask you for the numerator and denominator separately.

```
290 REM -----------------------------------------------
300 REM ROUTINE TO GENERATE NUMERATORS AND DENOMINATORS
310 REM -----------------------------------------------
320 N1=INT(RND(0)*LG)+1
330 N2=INT(RND(0)*LG)+1
340 D1=INT(RND(0)*LG)+1
350 D2=INT(RND(0)*LG)+1
360 IF N1/D1 >= N2/D2 THEN 390: REM ENSURE SUBT IS POS.
370 N3=N2:N2=N1:N1=N3: REM OTHERWISE SWAP
380 D3=D2:D2=D1:D1=D3
390 RETURN
410 REM ---------------------------------------
420 REM ROUTINE TO FIND GREATEST COMMON DENOMINATOR
430 REM ---------------------------------------
440 U=N3:V=D3
450 G=U-V*INT(U/V)
460 IF G=0 THEN RETURN
470 U=V:V=G
480 GOTO 450
500 REM ------------------------------
510 REM DISPLAY QUESTION AND GET ANSWER
520 REM ------------------------------
530 X=21:Y=5:GOSUB 4200: REM LOCATE
540 S1=3-LEN(STR$(N1)):S2=3-LEN(STR$(N2))
550 PRINT SPC(S1);N1;"  ";SPC(S2);N2
560 PRINT TAB(20);"--- ";SN$;" ---"
570 S1=3-LEN(STR$(D1)):S2=3-LEN(STR$(D2))
580 PRINT TAB(20);SPC(S1);D1;"  ";SPC(S2);D2
590 INPUT"TYPE NUMERATOR    ";AN
600 INPUT"TYPE DENOMINATOR  ";AD
610 PRINT:PRINT"CORRECT ANSWER IS: "
620 RETURN
650 REM -----------------------------
660 REM      FINISH THE PROBLEM
670 REM -----------------------------
680 S1=3-LEN(STR$(N3)):S2=3-LEN(STR$(D3))
690 PRINT TAB(20);SPC(S1);N3
700 PRINT TAB(20);"---"
710 PRINT TAB(20);SPC(S2);D3
720 S=0: IF AN=N3 AND AD=D3 THEN S=1
730 PRINT: PRINT"YOU ARE ";
740 IF S=1 THEN PRINT"RIGHT": R=R+1
750 IF S=0 THEN PRINT"WRONG": W=W+1
760 PRINT"PROBLEMS DONE";TAB(20);R+W
770 PRINT"CORRECT";TAB(20);R
780 PRINT"ERRORS";TAB(20);W
790 Q2$="PRACTICE":GOSUB 3400
800 RETURN
```

Figure 7.20: Program Listing: Fraction Subroutines

FRACTION ADDITION

Description

The Fraction Addition program allows you to practice adding two fractions. You select this program from the fraction program menu by striking the 1 on your keyboard. You must also enter the largest denominator you want to work with. (Don't be afraid of large denominators!)

Example

Figure 7.21 shows the addition of two fractions. Note that this is the second problem of a series. Figure 7.22 is the program listing for the addition drill.

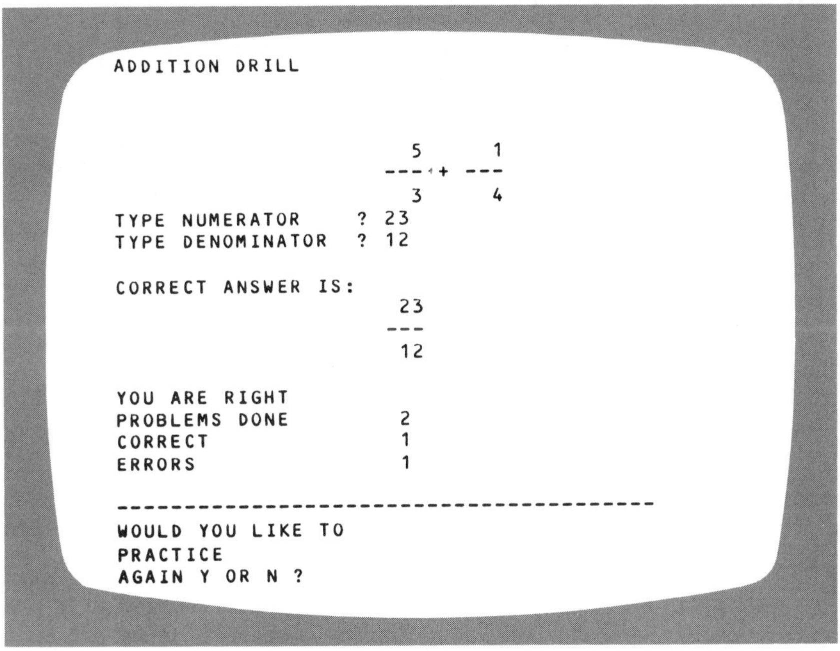

Figure 7.21: Screen Display: Fraction Addition

```
810 REM ------------------------------
820 N$=        "ADDITION DRILL"
830 REM ------------------------------
840 GOSUB 6200
850 GOSUB 290: REM GENERATE NUMS AND DENOMS
860 SN$="+"
870 GOSUB 500: REM DISP QUEST, GET ANS
880 N3=D2*N1+D1*N2: REM BEFORE CLEANUP
890 D3=D1*D2
900 REM FIND GREATEST COMMON DENOM
910 GOSUB 410
920 N3=N3/V:: D3=D3/V
930 GOSUB 650: REM FINISH UP
940 IF YN$="N" THEN RETURN
950 GOTO 810
```

Figure 7.22: Program Listing: Fraction Addition

FRACTION SUBTRACTION

Description

You can practice subtracting fractions with this program. You select the program by pressing 2 as you run the fraction drill menu. You also select the largest denominator you want to work with. Like the subtraction drill in the first menu, this program generates its numbers so that a positive answer always results.

Example

Figure 7.23 shows a screen display for the Fraction Subtraction program. Figure 7.24 is the program listing.

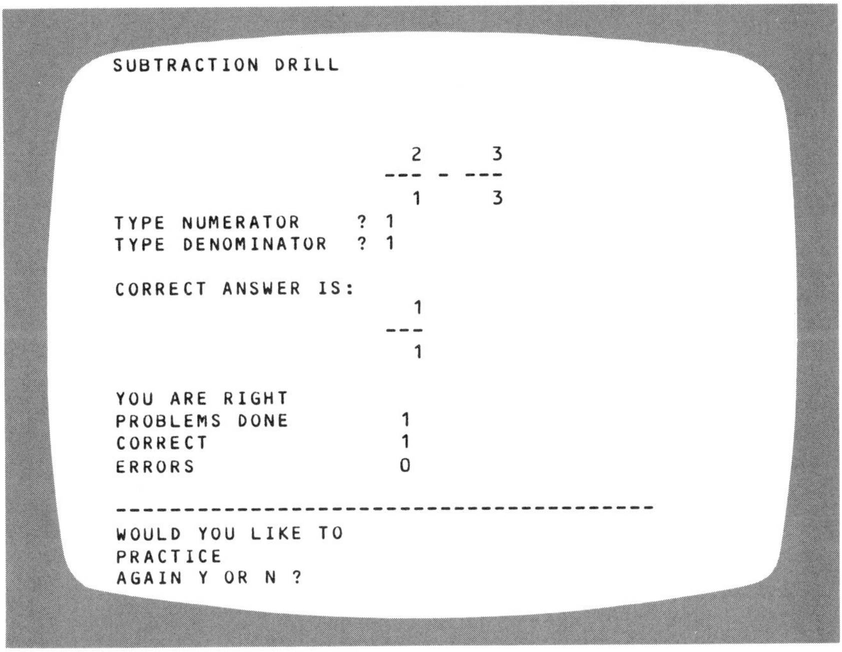

Figure 7.23: Screen Display: Fraction Subtraction

```
960 REM ------------------------------
970 N$=      "SUBTRACTION DRILL"
980 REM ------------------------------
990 GOSUB 6200
1000 GOSUB 290: REM GENERATE NUMS AND DENOMS
1010 N3=D2*N1-D1*N2: REM BEFORE CLEANUP
1020 IF N3=0 THEN 1000: REM DISALLOW 0
1030 SN$="-"
1040 GOSUB 500: REM DISP QUEST, GET ANS
1050 D3=D1*D2
1060 REM FIND GREATEST COMMON DENOM
1070 GOSUB 410
1080 N3=N3/V:D3=D3/V
1090 GOSUB 650: REM FINISH UP
1100 IF YN$="N" THEN RETURN
1110 GOTO 960
```

Figure 7.24: Program Listing: Fraction Subtraction

FRACTION MULTIPLICATION

Description

The Fraction Multiplication program allows you to practice multiplying two fractions. You select this program from the fraction menu by pressing the number 3. Fraction multiplication is very easy to learn, and it comes in handy—don't be afraid to try this drill.

Example

Figure 7.25 shows a screen display for the Fraction Multiplication program. Note that two out of four problems have been correctly answered. Figure 7.26 is the Fraction Multiplication program listing.

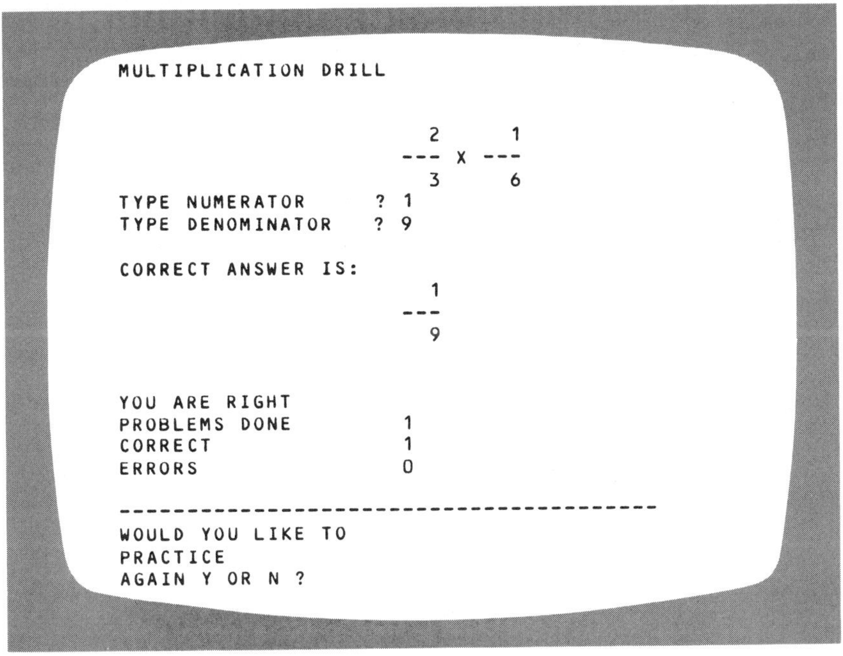

Figure 7.25: Screen Display: Fraction Multiplication

```
1120 REM -----------------------------
1130 N$=    "MULTIPLICATION DRILL"
1140 REM -----------------------------
1150 GOSUB 6200
1160 GOSUB 290: REM GENERATE NUMS AND DENOMS
1170 SN$="X"
1180 GOSUB 500: REM DISP QUEST, GET ANS
1190 N3=N1*N2:D3=D1*D2: REM BEFORE CLEANUP
1200 REM FIND GREATEST COMMON DENOM
1210 GOSUB 410
1220 N3=N3/V: D3=D3/V
1230 GOSUB 650: REM FINISH UP
1240 IF YN$="N" THEN RETURN
1250 GOTO 1120
```

Figure 7.26: Program Listing: Fraction Multiplication

FRACTION DIVISION

Description

The final fraction program allows you to practice dividing fractions. This program is chosen by pressing the 4 on your keyboard from the menu program. Dividing fractions is the same as multiplying fractions, except that you invert the second fraction (the denominator). Practice with this program will sharpen your skills and make fraction division a less formidable task for you.

Example

Figure 7.27 shows a screen display for the Fraction Division program. Figure 7.28 is the program listing.

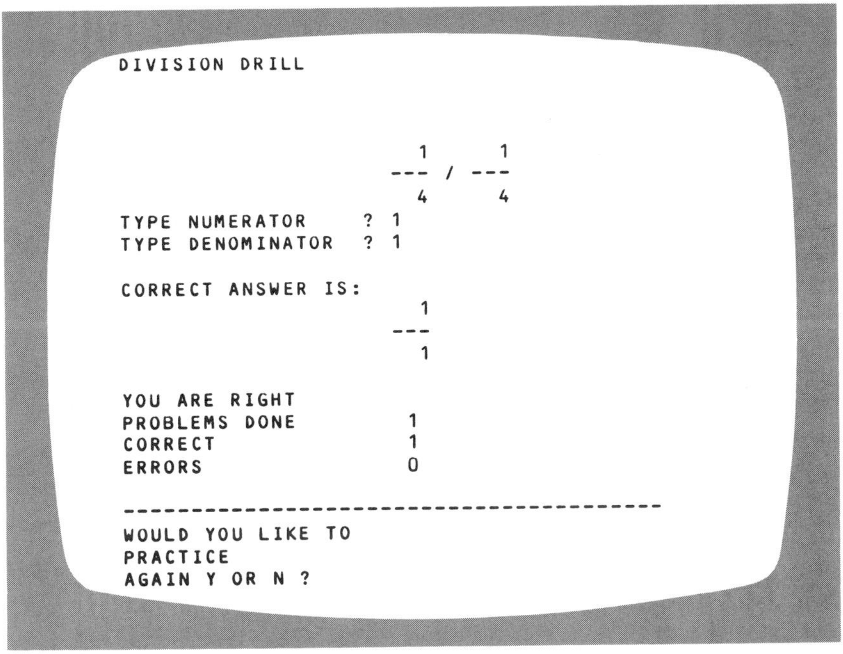

Figure 7.27: Screen Display: Fraction Division

```
1260 REM -----------------------------
1270 N$=        "DIVISION DRILL"
1280 REM -----------------------------
1290 GOSUB 6200
1300 GOSUB 290: REM GENERATE NUMS AND DENOMS
1310 N3=N1*D2:D3=D1*N2: REM BEFORE CLEANUP
1320 REM FIND GREATEST COMMON DENOM
1330 GOSUB 410
1340 N3=N3/V:D3=D3/V
1350 SN$="/"
1360 GOSUB 500: REM DISP QUEST, GET ANS
1370 GOSUB 650: REM FINISH UP
1380 IF YN$="N" THEN RETURN
1390 GOTO 1260
```

Figure 7.28: Program Listing: Fraction Division

A

CENTRAL SUBROUTINES

These subroutines allow us to create useful programs that are very short and thus easy to enter. Interested users should read Appendix B to see how these subroutines can be used in other applications.

This appendix contains the program listings for the central subroutines used throughout the book. The programs contain many remark statements to help you understand the functions of each subroutine.

You can save retyping these subroutines many times by saving them together in one file. Add them to your application programs as explained in Chapter 1. Remember that you need type only the first REM in each subroutine.

```
3000 REM          "SAVEFILE"
3010 REM -----------------------------
3020 REM      SAVE FILE TO DISK
3030 REM
3040 REM THIS ROUTINE SAVES FILE TO DISK
3050 REM
3060 REM CALLING PARAMETERS:
3065 REM    F$=NAME OF FILE TO SAVE TO
3070 REM    P$(N,8)=ARRAY OF DATA ITEMS
3080 REM    NR=NUMBER OF DATA ITEMS
3090 REM
3100 REM RETURNED PARAMETERS:
3110 REM    NONE
3120 REM
3130 REM -----------------------------
3140 A$="@0:"+F$+",SEQ,W"
3150 OPEN 2,8,2,A$
3155 PRINT# 2,NR
3160 FOR I=1 TO NR
3170 FOR J=1 TO 8
3180 PRINT# 2,P$(I,J)
3190 NEXT J
3200 NEXT I
3210 CLOSE 2
3220 RETURN
```

Figure A.1: Save File Subroutine

```
3400 REM           "ANOTH"
3401 REM -----------------------------
3402 REM      ASK FOR ANOTHER RUN
3403 REM
3404 REM THIS ROUTINE ASKS WHETHER TO CONTINUE
3405 REM
3406 REM CALLING PARAMETERS:
3407 REM     Q2$=SPECIFIES WHAT OPERATION TO DO
3408 REM
3409 REM RETURNED PARAMETERS:
3410 REM     YN$=A "Y" OR "N" FOR YES OR NO
3411 REM
3412 REM -----------------------------
3420 Q1$="WOULD YOU LIKE TO"
3430 Q3$="AGAIN Y OR N ?"
3440 GOSUB 5000: REM PRESENT DIALOG
3450 GOSUB 7800: REM ASK YES OR NO
3460 RETURN
```

Figure A.2: Request to Run Again Subroutine

```
3800 REM             "LOADFILE"
3810 REM -----------------------------
3820 REM   LOADS A FILE IN FROM DISK
3830 REM
3840 REM CALLING PARAMETERS:
3850 REM   F$=NAME OF FILE
3860 REM
3870 REM RETURNED PARAMETERS:
3880 REM   NR=NUMBER OF RECORDS IN FILE
3890 REM   P$(N,8)=DATA ITEMS
3900 REM
3910 REM -----------------------------
3920 A$="0:"+F$+",SEQ,R"
3930 OPEN 3,8,3,A$
3940 INPUT# 3,NR
3950 FOR I=1 TO NR
3960 FOR J=1 TO 8
3970 INPUT# 3,P$(I,J)
3980 NEXT J
3990 NEXT I
3995 CLOSE 3
4000 RETURN
```

Figure A.3: Load File Subroutine

```
4200 REM             "LOCATE"
4201 REM -----------------------------
4202 REM
4203 REM THIS ROUTINE MOVES THE CURSOR TO POSITION X,Y
4204 REM
4205 REM CALLING PARAMETERS:
4206 REM    X,Y=COORDINATES TO MOVE CURSOR
4207 REM
4208 REM RETURNED PARAMETERS:
4209 REM    NONE
4210 REM
4211 REM -----------------------------
4220 PRINT CHR$(19);:REM HOMES CURSOR
4225 IF X=1 THEN 4255
4230 FOR A=1 TO X-1
4240 PRINT CHR$(29);:REM CURSOR RIGHT
4250 NEXT A
4255 IF Y=1 THEN 4290
4260 FOR A=1 TO Y-1
4270 PRINT CHR$(17);:REM CURSOR DOWN
4280 NEXT A
4290 RETURN
```

Figure A.4: Move Cursor Subroutine

```
5000 REM        "DIALOG"
5001 REM -----------------------------
5002 REM        DIALOGUE
5003 REM
5004 REM CALLING PARAMETERS:
5005 REM    Q1$,Q2$,Q3$=QUESTIONS TO DISPLAY
5006 REM
5007 REM RETURNED PARAMETERS:
5008 REM    NONE
5009 REM
5010 REM COMMENT:  UNUSED CHARACTER STRINGS
5011 REM    SHOULD BE SET TO NULL ( "" )
5012 REM
5013 REM -----------------------------
5020 X=1:Y=21:GOSUB 4200: REM LOCATE
5030 PRINT D$;S$:PRINT S$:PRINT S$;
5040 X=1:Y=22:GOSUB 4200
5050 PRINT Q1$:PRINT Q2$:PRINT Q3$;
5060 RETURN
```

Figure A.5: Diplay Dialog Subroutine

```
5400 REM         "INCH"
5401 REM -----------------------------
5402 REM      INPUT CHARACTER
5403 REM
5404 REM CALLING PARAMETERS:
5405 REM    NONE
5406 REM
5407 REM RETURNED PARAMETERS:
5408 REM    CH$=INPUT CHARACTER
5409 REM
5410 REM -----------------------------
5420 GET CH$
5430 IF CH$="" THEN 5420
5440 RETURN
```

Figure A.6: Input Character Subroutine

```
6200 REM           "INIT"
6201 REM -----------------------------
6202 REM     INITIALIZE DISPLAY
6203 REM
6204 REM THIS ROUTINE CLEARS THE SCREEN
6205 REM    AND PRINTS THE PROGRAM TITLE
6206 REM CALLING PARAMETERS:
6207 REM    N$=TITLE OF PROGRAM
6208 REM
6209 REM RETURNED PARAMETERS:
6210 REM    NONE
6211 REM
6212 REM -----------------------------
6220 PRINT CHR$(147);:REM CLEAR SCREEN
6230 PRINT N$: PRINT: REM PROGRAM TITLE
6240 S$="                                        "
6250 D$="----------------------------------------"
6260 RETURN
```

Figure A.7: Initialize Program and Display Subroutine

```
6600 REM           "INPAR"
6601 REM -----------------------------
6602 REM       INPUT PARAMETERS
6603 REM
6604 REM CALLING PARAMETERS:
6605 REM    Q1$,Q2$=USER INSTRUCTIONS
6606 REM    Q3$=NAME OF DATA ITEM
6607 REM
6608 REM RETURNED PARAMETERS:
6609 REM    P(K)=THE DATA ITEM OBTAINED
6610 REM
6611 REM COMMENT: CALL WITH K=1 FOR FIRST DATA ITEM
6612 REM          K UPDATED AUTOMATICALLY
6613 REM
6614 REM -----------------------------
6620 GOSUB 5000: REM ASK QUESTIONS
6630 INPUT P(K): REM GET VALUE
6640 REM ECHO QUESTION AND ANSWER
6650 X=3: Y=K+2:GOSUB 4200: REM LOCATE
6660 PRINT Q3$;TAB(24);P(K)
6670 K=K+1
6680 RETURN
```

Figure A.8: Input Program Parameters Subroutine

```
7000 REM              "MENU"
7001 REM -----------------------------
7002 REM           MENU PROGRAM
7003 REM
7004 REM THIS PROGRAM DISPLAYS A MENU
7005 REM    AND CHOOSES A PROGRAM
7006 REM CALLING PARAMETERS:
7007 REM    N=NO. OF MENU ITEMS
7008 REM    X$(I)=ARRAY OF PROGRAM NAMES
7009 REM
7010 REM RETURNED PARAMETERS:
7011 REM    X=PROGRAM NUMBER CHOSEN
7012 REM
7013 REM -----------------------------
7020 PRINT CHR$(147);:REM CLEAR SCREEN
7030 FOR I=1 TO N
7040 IF I<10 THEN PRINT I;
7050 IF I=10 THEN PRINT 0;
7060 PRINT"= ";X$(I)
7070 NEXT I
7080 Q1$="":Q2$=""
7090 Q3$="CHOOSE PROGRAM: "
7100 GOSUB 5000: REM ASK QUESTIONS
7110 GOSUB 5400: REM INPUT CHAR
7120 X=VAL(CH$)
7130 IF X=0 THEN X=10
7140 REM SEE IF CHAR IN RANGE
7150 IF X>=1 AND X<=N THEN RETURN
7160 Q1$="ILLEGAL CHOICE, CHOOSE AGAIN"
7170 GOTO 7100
```

Figure A.9: Display Menu Subroutine

```
7400 REM              "PAUSE"
7401 REM -----------------------------
7402 REM         WAIT FOR ANY KEY
7403 REM
7404 REM THIS ROUTINE WAITS FOR THE USER TO STRIKE KEY
7405 REM
7406 REM CALLING PARAMETERS:
7407 REM    NONE
7408 REM
7409 REM RETURNED PARAMETERS:
7410 REM    NONE
7411 REM
7412 REM -----------------------------
7420 Q1$="STRIKE ANY KEY TO CONTINUE"
7430 Q2$="":Q3$=""
7440 GOSUB 5000: REM CALL DIALOG
7450 GET X$: IF X$="" THEN 7450
7460 RETURN
```

Figure A.10: Pause Subroutine

```
7800 REM              "YESNO"
7801 REM -----------------------------
7802 REM              YES-NO
7803 REM
7804 REM CALLING PARAMETERS:
7805 REM    NONE
7806 REM
7807 REM RETURNED PARAMETERS:
7808 REM    YN$=CONTAINS A  Y OR N
7809 REM
7810 REM -----------------------------
7820 REM WAIT FOR KEY TO BE STRUCK
7830 GET YN$: IF YN$="" THEN 7830
7840 IF YN$<>"Y" AND YN$<>"N" THEN 7830
7850 PRINT YN$: RETURN
```

Figure A.11: Yes or No Subroutine

B

HOW TO USE THE CENTRAL SUBROUTINES

Readers who would like to improve their programming skills should try writing their own programs. You can save a lot of time and effort by using the central subroutines in this book as part of your programs. This appendix will help you learn to use these central subroutines. We review here several of the subroutines and how they function. We also include sample programs that show how the subroutines can be used.

MENU SET-UP

The menu set-up subroutine begins at line 7000. This subroutine displays a menu on the screen and waits for the user to press a number key. The menu program then returns a value, which you use to select the program you want to run.

Figures B.1 and B.2 show the program listing and screen display for a sample menu selection. We set up the array X$(I) with the names of the available programs. We then set N= to the number of program choices and call the menu subroutine. The subroutine displays the names of the programs and waits for the user to make a selection. The subroutine then returns the value of the selected program. The returned value is used in a GOSUB statement to select a program.

```
100 REM -----------------------------
110 N$=      "MENU DEMONSTRATION"
120 REM -----------------------------
130 GOSUB 6200: REM INITIALIZE
140 REM SET UP MENU ARRAY
150 X$(1)="PROGRAM 1"
160 X$(2)="PROGRAM 2"
170 X$(3)="PROGRAM 3"
180 X$(4)="PROGRAM 4"
190 N=4: GOSUB 7000: REM DISPLAY MENU
200 ON X GOTO 210,220,230,240: REM SELECT PROGRAM
210 PRINT "PROGRAM 1 CHOSEN": END
220 PRINT "PROGRAM 2 CHOSEN": END
230 PRINT "PROGRAM 3 CHOSEN": END
240 PRINT "PROGRAM 4 CHOSEN": END
```

Figure B.1: Program Listing: Sample Menu Selection

```
1 = PROGRAM 1
2 = PROGRAM 2
3 = PROGRAM 3
4 = PROGRAM 4

----------------------------------------

CHOOSE PROGRAM:
```

Figure B.2: Screen Display: Sample Menu Selection

CHOOSING ANOTHER PROGRAM

All the programs in this book use the ANOTH subroutine. This subroutine asks the user whether he would like to run the program again. The subroutine displays three lines of data. The ANOTH subroutine generates the first and third data lines. You specify the second line when you call the subroutine.

The ANOTH routine returns a Y or an N in the variable YN$. The program tests this variable to decide whether it will run the program again.

Figures B.3 and B.4 show the program listing and a screen display for the ANOTH demonstration. Note that the sample program displays the question DEMONSTRATE THIS ROUTINE.

```
250 REM ------------------------------
260 N$= "DEMO OF 'ANOTHER' SUBROUTINE"
270 REM ------------------------------
280 GOSUB 6200: REM INITIALIZE
290 Q2$="DEMONSTRATE THIS ROUTINE"
300 GOSUB 3400: REM ASK FOR ANOTHER
310 IF YN$="Y" THEN 250
320 END
```

Figure B.3: Program Listing: Demonstration of ANOTH Subroutine

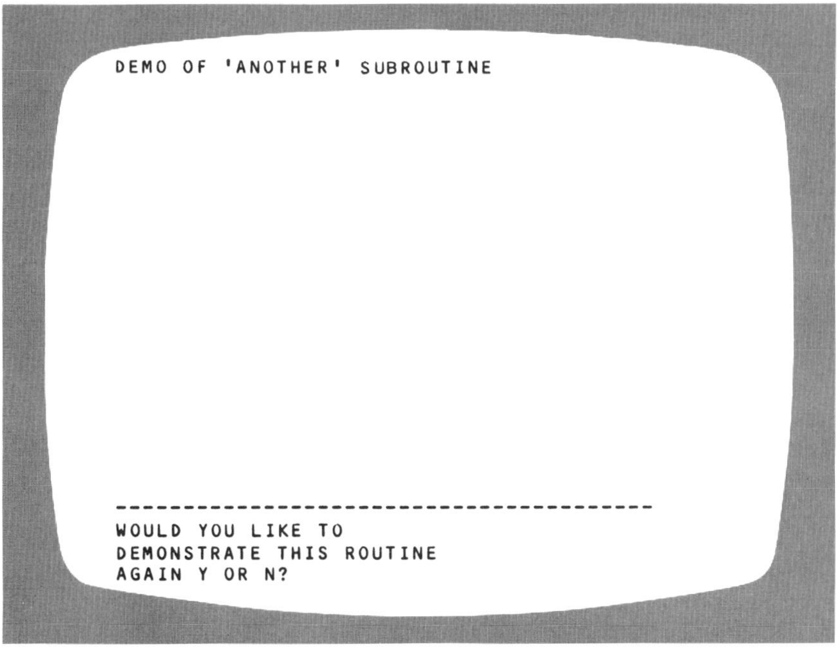

Figure B.4: Screen Display: Demonstration of ANOTH Subroutine

THE DIALOG SUBROUTINE

We use the DIALOG subroutine to display three lines of text at the bottom of the screen. You have the flexibility to generate three different questions; three questions or instructions will handle most programs you design. We often give an instruction on the first line, with questions on the second and third lines. This routine also draws a border and clears leftover text from previous questions. The routine exits with the cursor after the third question. Figures B.5 and B.6 show a program listing and screen display of a DIALOG demonstration.

```
330 REM ------------------------------
340 N$= "DEMO OF 'DIALOG' SUBROUTINE"
350 REM ------------------------------
360 GOSUB 6200: REM INITIALIZE
370 REM SET UP QUESTIONS
380 Q1$="THIS IS THE FIRST QUESTION"
390 Q2$="": REM A BLANK QUESTION
400 Q3$="THIS IS THE LAST QUESTION"
410 GOSUB 5000: REM SEND OUT QUESTIONS
420 END
```

Figure B.5: Program Listing: Demonstration of DIALOG Subroutine

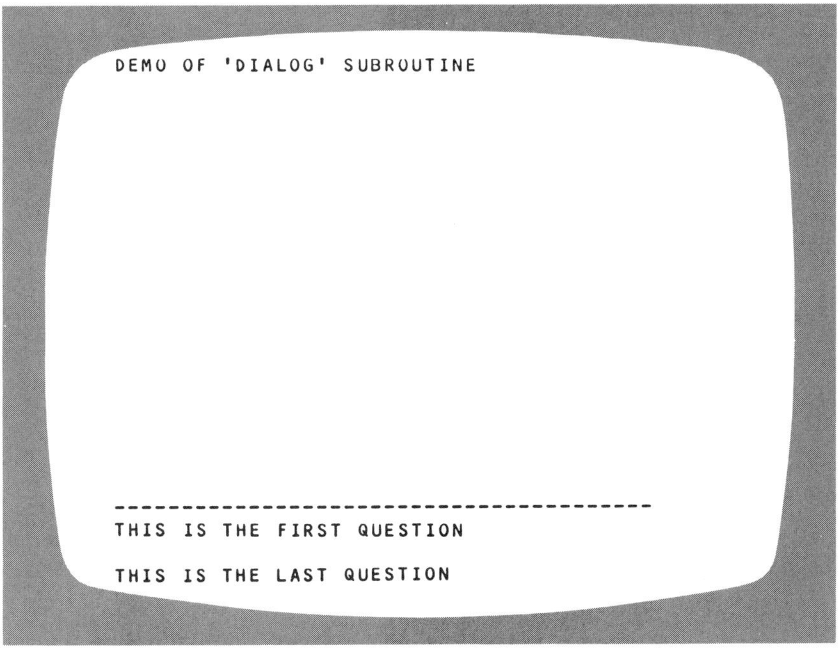

Figure B.6: Screen Display: Demonstration of DIALOG Subroutine

DATA INPUT SUBROUTINE

The INPAR program handles data input for many of the programs in this book and is easily used to create additional programs. You begin the data input process by clearing the screen with the INIT subroutine and setting the index K equal to 1. You are now ready to input program parameters. For each parameter, set Q3$ equal to the name of the parameter and call the subroutine at 6600. The INPAR subroutine asks the parameter name at the bottom of the screen and waits for input. The parameter then appears at the top of the screen. INPAR stores parameters in the array P(K) in the order of entry. Figures B.7 and B.8 show a program listing and screen display of the Data Input program.

```
430 REM ------------------------------
440 N$=   "DATA INPUT DEMONSTRATION"
450 REM ------------------------------
460 GOSUB 6200: K=1: REM INITIALIZE
470 REM SET UP DIALOG AREA
480 Q1$="ENTER DATA":Q2$=""
490 Q3$="RETAIL PRICE ($)": GOSUB 6600: REM 1ST ITEM
500 Q3$="DISCOUNT (%)":GOSUB 6600: REM GET 2ND ITEM
510 PRINT: PRINT"PRICE = ";TAB(22);
520 P=P(1)-P(2)/100*P(1)
530 P=INT(P*100+.5)/100: REM ROUND OFF TO TWO PLACES
540 PRINT P
550 END
```

Figure B.7: Program Listing: Data Input Demonstration

```
DATA INPUT DEMONSTRATION

  RETAIL PRICE ($)       300
  DISCOUNT (%)           10

PRICE =                 270

READY.











----------------------------------------
ENTER DATA

DISCOUNT (%)? 10
```

Figure B.8: Screen Display: Data Input Demonstration

The SYBEX Library

Buyer's Guide

THE BEST OF TI 99/4A™ CARTRIDGES

by Thomas Blackadar

150 pp., illustr., Ref. 0-137

Save yourself time and frustration when buying TI 99/4A software. This buyer's guide gives an overview of the best available programs, with information on how to set up the computer to run them.

FAMILY COMPUTERS UNDER $200

by Doug Mosher

160 pp., illustr., Ref. 0-149

Find out what these inexpensive machines can do for you and your family. "If you're just getting started . . . this is the book to read before you buy."—Richard O'Reilly, Los Angeles newspaper columnist

PORTABLE COMPUTERS

by Sheldon Crop and Doug Mosher

128 pp., illustr., Ref. 0-144

"This book provides a clear and concise introduction to the expanding new world of personal computers."—Mark Powelson, Editor, San Francisco Focus Magazine

THE BEST OF VIC-20™ SOFTWARE

by Thomas Blackadar

150 pp., illustr., Ref. 0-139

Save yourself time and frustration with this buyer's guide to VIC-20 software. Find the best game, music, education, and home management programs on the market today.

SELECTING THE RIGHT DATA BASE SOFTWARE

SELECTING THE RIGHT WORD PROCESSING SOFTWARE

SELECTING THE RIGHT SPREADSHEET SOFTWARE

by Kathy McHugh and Veronica Corchado

80 pp., illustr., Ref. 0-174, 0-177, 0-178

This series on selecting the right business software offers the busy professional concise, informative reviews of the best available software packages.

Introduction to Computers

OVERCOMING COMPUTER FEAR

by Jeff Berner

112 pp., illustr., Ref. 0-145

This easy-going introduction to computers helps you separate the facts from the myths.

COMPUTER ABC'S

by Daniel Le Noury and Rodnay Zaks

64 pp., illustr., Ref. 0-167

This beautifully illustrated, colorful book for parents and children takes you alphabetically through the world of computers, explaining each concept in simple language.

PARENTS, KIDS, AND COMPUTERS
by Lynn Alpers and Meg Holmberg
208 pp., illustr., Ref. 0-151
This book answers your questions about the educational possibilities of home computers.

THE COLLEGE STUDENT'S COMPUTER HANDBOOK
by Bryan Pfaffenberger
350 pp., illustr., Ref. 0-170
This friendly guide will aid students in selecting a computer system for college study, managing information in a college course, and writing research papers.

COMPUTER CRAZY
by Daniel Le Noury
100 pp., illustr., Ref. 0-173
No matter how you feel about computers, these cartoons will have you laughing about them.

DON'T!
(or How to Care for Your Computer)
by Rodnay Zaks
214pp., 100 illustr., Ref. 0-065
The correct way to handle and care for all elements of a computer system, including what to do when something doesn't work.

YOUR FIRST COMPUTER
by Rodnay Zaks
258 pp., 150 illustr., Ref. 0-045
The most popular introduction to small computers and their peripherals: what they do and how to buy one.

INTERNATIONAL MICROCOMPUTER DICTIONARY
120 pp., Ref. 0-067
All the definitions and acronyms of microcomputer jargon defined in a handy pocket-sized edition. Includes translations of the most popular terms into ten languages.

FROM CHIPS TO SYSTEMS: AN INTRODUCTION TO MICROPROCESSORS
by Rodnay Zaks
552 pp., 400 illustr., Ref. 0-063
A simple and comprehensive introduction to microprocessors from both a hardware and software standpoint: what they are, how they operate, how to assemble them into a complete system.

Personal Computers

ATARI

YOUR FIRST ATARI® PROGRAM
by Rodnay Zaks
150 pp., illustr., Ref. 0-130
A fully illustrated, easy-to-use introduction to ATARI BASIC programming. Will have the reader programming in a matter of hours.

BASIC EXERCISES FOR THE ATARI®
by J.P. Lamoitier
251 pp., illustr., Ref. 0-101
Teaches ATARI BASIC through actual practice using graduated exercises drawn from everyday applications.

THE EASY GUIDE TO YOUR ATARI® 600XL/800XL
by Thomas Blackadar
175 pp., illustr., Ref. 0-125
This jargon-free companion will help you get started on the right foot with your new 600XL or 800XL ATARI computer.

ATARI® BASIC PROGRAMS IN MINUTES
by Stanley R. Trost
170 pp., illustr., Ref. 0-143
You can use this practical set of programs without any prior knowledge of BASIC! Application examples are taken from a wide variety of fields, including business, home management, and real estate.

Commodore 64/VIC-20

THE COMMODORE 64™/VIC-20™ BASIC HANDBOOK

by Douglas Hergert

144 pp., illustr., Ref. 0-116

A complete listing with descriptions and instructive examples of each of the Commodore 64 BASIC keywords and functions. A handy reference guide, organized like a dictionary.

THE EASY GUIDE TO YOUR COMMODORE 64™

by Joseph Kascmer

160 pp., illustr., Ref. 0-129

A friendly introduction to using the Commodore 64.

YOUR FIRST VIC-20™ PROGRAM

by Rodnay Zaks

150 pp., illustr., Ref. 0-129

A fully illustrated, easy-to-use introduction to VIC-20 BASIC programming. Will have the reader programming in a matter of hours.

THE VIC-20™ CONNECTION

by James W. Coffron

260 pp., 120 illustr., Ref. 0-128

Teaches elementary interfacing and BASIC programming of the VIC-20 for connection to external devices and household appliances.

YOUR FIRST COMMODORE 64™ PROGRAM

by Rodnay Zaks

182 pp., illustr., Ref. 0-172

You can learn to write simple programs without any prior knowledge of mathematics or computers! Guided by colorful illustrations and step-by-step instructions, you'll be constructing programs within an hour or two.

COMMODORE 64™ BASIC PROGRAMS IN MINUTES

by Stanley R. Trost

170 pp., illustr., Ref. 0-154

Here is a practical set of programs for business, finance, real estate, data analysis, record keeping and educational applications.

GRAPHICS GUIDE TO THE COMMODORE 64™

by Charles Platt

192 pp., illustr., Ref. 0-138

This easy-to-understand book will appeal to anyone who wants to master the Commodore 64's powerful graphics features.

Software and Applications

Operating Systems

THE CP/M® HANDBOOK

by Rodnay Zaks

320 pp., 100 illustr., Ref 0-048

An indispensable reference and guide to CP/M—the most widely-used operating system for small computers.

MASTERING CP/M®

by Alan R. Miller

398 pp., illustr., Ref. 0-068

For advanced CP/M users or systems programmers who want maximum use of the CP/M operating system . . . takes up where our *CP/M Handbook* leaves off.

THE BEST OF CP/M® SOFTWARE

by John D. Halamka

250 pp., illustr., Ref. 0-100

This book reviews tried-and-tested, commercially available software for your CP/M system.

REAL WORLD UNIX

by John D. Halamka

250 pp., illustr., Ref. 0-093

This book is written for the beginning and intermediate UNIX user in a practical, straightforward manner, with specific instructions given for many special applications.

THE CP/M PLUS™ HANDBOOK
by Alan R. Miller
250 pp., illustr., Ref. 0-158
This guide is easy for the beginner to understand, yet contains valuable information for advanced users of CP/M Plus (Version 3).

Business Software

INTRODUCTION TO WORDSTAR™
by Arthur Naiman
202 pp., 30 illustr., Ref. 0-077
Makes it easy to learn how to use WordStar, a powerful word processing program for personal computers.

PRACTICAL WORDSTAR™ USES
by Julie Anne Arca
200 pp., illustr., Ref. 0-107
Pick your most time-consuming office tasks and this book will show you how to streamline them with WordStar.

MASTERING VISICALC®
by Douglas Hergert
217 pp., 140 illustr., Ref. 0-090
Explains how to use the VisiCalc "electronic spreadsheet" functions and provides examples of each. Makes using this powerful program simple.

DOING BUSINESS WITH VISICALC®
by Stanley R. Trost
260 pp., Ref. 0-086
Presents accounting and management planning applications—from financial statements to master budgets; from pricing models to investment strategies.

DOING BUSINESS WITH SUPERCALC™
by Stanley R. Trost
248 pp., illustr., Ref. 0-095
Presents accounting and management planning applications—from financial statements to master budgets; from pricing models to investment strategies.

VISICALC® FOR SCIENCE AND ENGINEERING
by Stanley R. Trost and Charles Pomernacki
225 pp., illustr., Ref. 0-096
More than 50 programs for solving technical problems in the science and engineering fields. Applications range from math and statistics to electrical and electronic engineering.

DOING BUSINESS WITH 1-2-3™
by Stanley R. Trost
250 pp., illustr., Ref. 0-159
If you are a business professional using the 1-2-3 software package, you will find the spreadsheet and graphics models provided in this book easy to use "as is" in everyday business situations.

THE ABC'S OF 1-2-3™
by Chris Gilbert
225 pp., illustr., Ref. 0-168
For those new to the LOTUS 1-2-3 program, this book offers step-by-step instructions in mastering its spreadsheet, data base, and graphing capabilities.

UNDERSTANDING dBASE II™
by Alan Simpson
220 pp., illustr., Ref. 0-147
Learn programming techniques for mailing label systems, bookkeeping and data base management, as well as ways to interface dBASE II with other software systems.

DOING BUSINESS WITH dBASE II™
by Stanley R. Trost
250 pp., illustr., Ref. 0-160
Learn to use dBASE II for accounts receivable, recording business income and expenses, keeping personal records and mailing lists, and much more.

BASIC FOR BUSINESS

by Douglas Hergert

224 pp., 15 illustr., Ref. 0-080

A logically organized, no-nonsense introduction to BASIC programming for business applications. Includes many fully-explained accounting programs, and shows you how to write them.

EXECUTIVE PLANNING WITH BASIC

by X. T. Bui

196 pp., 19 illustr., Ref. 0-083

An important collection of business management decision models in BASIC, including Inventory Management (EOQ), Critical Path Analysis and PERT, Financial Ratio Analysis, Portfolio Management, and much more.

BASIC PROGRAMS FOR SCIENTISTS AND ENGINEERS

by Alan R. Miller

318 pp., 120 illustr., Ref. 0-073

This book from the "Programs for Scientists and Engineers" series provides a library of problem-solving programs while developing proficiency in BASIC.

CELESTIAL BASIC

by Eric Burgess

300 pp., 65 illustr., Ref. 0-087

A collection of BASIC programs that rapidly complete the chores of typical astronomical computations. It's like having a planetarium in your own home! Displays apparent movement of stars, planets and meteor showers.

YOUR SECOND BASIC PROGRAM

by Gary Lippman

250 pp., illustr., Ref. 0-152

A sequel to *Your First BASIC Program*, this book follows the same patient, detailed approach and brings you to the next level of programming skill.

Pascal

INTRODUCTION TO PASCAL (Including UCSD Pascal™)

by Rodnay Zaks

420 pp., 130 illustr., Ref. 0-066

A step-by-step introduction for anyone wanting to learn the Pascal language. Describes UCSD and Standard Pascals. No technical background is assumed.

THE PASCAL HANDBOOK

by Jacques Tiberghien

486 pp., 270 illustr., Ref. 0-053

A dictionary of the Pascal language, defining every reserved word, operator, procedure and function found in all major versions of Pascal.

APPLE® PASCAL GAMES

by Douglas Hergert and Joseph T. Kalash

372 pp., 40 illustr., Ref. 0-074

A collection of the most popular computer games in Pascal, challenging the reader not only to play but to investigate how games are implemented on the computer.

INTRODUCTION TO THE UCSD p-SYSTEM™

by Charles W. Grant and Jon Butah

300 pp., 10 illustr., Ref. 0-061

A simple, clear introduction to the UCSD Pascal Operating System; for beginners through experienced programmers.

PASCAL PROGRAMS FOR SCIENTISTS AND ENGINEERS

by Alan R. Miller

374 pp., 120 illustr., Ref. 0-058

A comprehensive collection of frequently used algorithms for scientific and technical applications, programmed in Pascal. Includes such programs as curve-fitting, integrals and statistical techniques.

Hardware and Peripherals

MICROPROCESSOR INTERFACING TECHNIQUES
by Rodnay Zaks and Austin Lesea
456 pp., 400 illustr., Ref. 0-029
Complete hardware and software interconnect techniques, including D to A conversion, peripherals, standard buses and troubleshooting.

THE RS-232 SOLUTION
by Joe Campbell
225 pp., illustr., Ref. 0-140
Finally, a book that will show you how to correctly interface your computer to any RS-232-C peripheral.

USING CASSETTE RECORDERS WITH COMPUTERS
by James Richard Cook
175 pp., illustr., Ref. 0-169
Whatever your computer or application, you will find this book helpful in explaining details of cassette care and maintenance.